CW00330512

TRENT

Part Two, 1946-68

By
David Bean

ROBIN HOOD PUBLISHING

ATTENBOROUGH, NOTTS

To
Michael and Jenny

All rights reserved. Except for normal review purposes, no part of this book may be reproduced or utilised in any form, or by any means, electrical or mechanical, including photocopying, recording, or by an information storage and retrieval system, without the prior written consent of Robin Hood Publishing.

Other Transport Titles by the Publisher:

Barton (Part Two, 1950-1961)
Barton (Part Three, 1962-1989)
South Notts
Hulley's
Trent (Part One, 1905-1945)
Midland General
West Bridgford UDC

Front Cover Photograph

Buses were still operating off Ilkeston Market Place when Peter Yeomans took this photograph in the early seventies. The vehicle, 224, ACH 224B was one of eight Leyland Leopards delivered to Trent in 1962. The bodywork was Alexander's Y type, with 49 seats, but although to coach specification, the business-like appearance meant that Trent numbered the vehicles in their dual-purpose, or semi-coach series. The vehicles were extensively used on the Company's seasonal express and middle distance services, and also on the Nottingham-London service of United Counties, after Trent took on local control responsibility for that service from 1963. However, 224 is seen here laying over after a short run on the service from Derby to Ilkeston.

Designed and Published by

PUBLISHING
Attenborough

TRENT

Part Two, 1946-68

CONTENTS

ISBN 0 948854 14 6

© April, 2002 David Bean

Foreword

This second volume of David Bean's story covers a period within the working memory of a number of current and recently retired Trent people.

These were the days of the federal structure of the BET Group where individuality was encouraged and pride in one's company was strong. Markedly different identities and liveries were much in evidence amongst the BET subsidiaries.

Trent was never a jewel in the BET crown like say, Ribble or Southdown, but it was a good solid company and a rung on the ladder for many managers destined for the top.

This period saw passenger carryings peak in the immediate post war years and then start the steady decline of some 2% or 3% per annum which continued until relatively recently.

Being a Londoner I only ever saw the odd Trent coach in my early years so imagine my delight when double deck 1038 arrived in Victoria Coach Station to show off its illuminated adverts. (see the picture on page 31).

Then the BET Senior Management Training Scheme took me to North Western - joint operator with Trent of Services 4, X1 and X2.

It was on World Cup Day 1966, that I drove my first Trent bus (a 2 speed axle Leopard dual purpose, actually) on the X2. North Western's Manchester depot had a duty which, although doing a Nottingham return trip, never touched a North Western vehicle as it was the middle section of the Blackpool (X60) to Great Yarmouth (X7) through running. So mine was a Ribble southbound and a Trent northbound There were conductors on express services in those days and separate tickets were issued for the X2, X7 and X60 sections. Imagine getting on with a large family - you'd be able to paper the walls!

My first recollection of Nottingham was the glorious smell of the bacon butties in Kent Street canteen - something which stays with you forever.

Whilst at North Western I appeared in Traffic Court to give evidence in favour of the joint Trent/North Western/LUT application for a Nottingham - Liverpool service as part of the build up of express services which this book describes.

Someone must have thought that I'd learned something about those two cities because I moved first to Liverpool with Ribble and then to Nottingham to become Trent's District Traffic Superintendent in 1968. This was within months of nationalisation and the end of this volume of David Bean's book. Thus many of the vehicles, services and garages described in the book have meant a lot to me for nearly 40 years.

David has continued his long quest to record the progress of this great company and in so doing his work will appeal to serious transport and social historians. However, as it covers the immediate post war period through to the late sixties, it will also appeal to those who have found Trent in more recent times and those whose lives have been inextricably bound up in the Company and the events associated with it.

Trent today is recognised as a market leader in its investment, innovation, marketing and training. We are providing enough material to keep David busy producing successor volumes for many years to come!

Brian King
Managing Director
Trent Buses

Introduction

When Part One of this history was published, I reflected on my research and realised that it had been a privilege to meet many people and share time with them hearing of their stories and experience, and also to have access to Company records and premises. It was also a privilege to set the information down for others to share, and now again to offer this second volume. I felt a little trepidation when Part One was published, but I have been very gratified by the generous reaction, and much encouraged to press on with the next part.

I had intended that Part Two would cover the period from 1946 until privatisation of the Company in 1986. However, having almost completed that work, it became evident that there was too much material to include in a single volume, and it would have to be split. Logically, therefore, Part Two takes the story to the end of the BET era, when the Company was sold to the government, an event which began in 1967, but was not fully effected until the first part of 1968. Part Three will cover the period from the second part of 1968 until the end of National Bus Company ownership in 1986 - a remarkably eventful period, despite at first sight seeming to be a period of considerable uniformity. A further volume will cover the very interesting story of the Company's subsequent development in private ownership.

I was born in 1948, and took an early interest in railways, but was soon introduced to the buses of Trent which my family and I used, to get from Allestree, where we lived, into Derby for shopping, or to Nottingham, where we had relations to visit. The first new buses that I think I can remember arriving were the DRC registered batch of Leyland bodied PD2s. I didn't know at the time that that was what they were, but as they arrived in 1953, I obviously became hooked as an enthusiast from a very early age.

This book is really about my era of Trent. I greatly enjoyed working on Part One and finding out about all the events that had made Trent the company that had drawn my interest, but I had no first hand knowledge. Although I can remember the rebodied Daimler COG5s and the utility Daimlers reasonably well I thought, at the time, that they were old crocks and should be instantly replaced with more new Leylands! Now, I'd jump at a ride on a COG5, and all the Leylands have gone, too.

When I began to take an interest, much of the fleet had been updated, after the war, and really looked quite modern, for there were only 47 spartan looking utility Daimlers, although some of the first post war rebodies also looked a little basic, too. The Company had just entered a period of transition from front engine to underfloor engine single deckers. It had also just passed the end of the golden years and traffic was beginning to decline with the social changes brought about by the car, and increasing affluence of the population. Costs were rising, and the industry entered a period of twin pressures from rising costs and falling traffic. I didn't realise all this at that time, although I can clearly remember stickers inside the buses, complaining about the continued rise in the level of road fuel tax.

My favourite vehicles of the time were the Willowbrook bodied PD3s which arrived in 1958. I hadn't known they were on order, and I still clearly remember the first one I saw, on the Belper 2, coming up the hill into Allestree from Duffield. They looked so big, held 73 passengers, and made a wonderful deep rorty exhaust note.

We left Allestree in 1959, to live in Croydon, where it was all red RTs (well, I admit there were a few green ones too, but they were still RTs!) and I thought rather boring. On my next return visit to Derby, the first Atlanteans had arrived, and these were something quite different, but why didn't we have them where I now lived? It was to be several years until London Transport bought any. Buses continued to get bigger, and in 1963, I made one of my regular visits and saw the first 36ft Leopards with attractive BET style bodies in the almost unique Trent dual purpose livery style - they too were favourite vehicles. Trent later turned away from Atlanteans to Daimler Fleetlines, and a regular pattern was set of Daimler Fleetline deckers and Leyland Leopard buses, dps and coaches.

I was delighted when Trent began, at last, to run into London's Victoria Coach Station, not only on the Derbyshire Express, but also on hire to United Counties for their London-Nottingham service, which I always thought should have been a Trent service anyway! It wasn't a political thing, but I was most concerned when BET sold their bus interests to the government, for I was convinced that all buses would be Bristols and painted Tilling red or Tilling green. I wasn't quite right about that, but I was definitely on the right track with the idea. So, at that point, this volume ends, and the story of Trent as a part of the National Bus Company, and its buses donning the same livery as many other companies, will be told in the next volume. However, as I write this, Trent has quite recently been voted Bus Operator of the Year for the second time, with runner-up in between. Now, my favourite bus company is everyone else's favourite, too!

David Bean
Buntingford, Hertfordshire.   April 2002

Typical of the appearance of new and rebodied double deckers in the fleet during the period covered by Chapter one is 1043, RC 4649, a 1937 AEC Regent with Willowbrook H56R body fitted in 1948. It was photographed the following year in Nottingham, and remained in the fleet until 1958, being renumbered 1168 in 1957. The presence of the suitcase is intriguing!

Post War Renewal and Reinstatement 1946-50

The first volume of this story told of the Company's development from the origins of the Commercial Car Company in 1905, through to the formation of Commercial Car Hirers, Ltd (CCHL), in 1909. This subsidiary company was the forerunner of Trent, and started its first service in Derbyshire, between Ashbourne and Derby, in September 1909. This was followed by several other services, until there was a total of six, in 1913. The British Automobile Traction Co, Ltd (BAT), a subsidiary of the British Electric Traction Co, Ltd (BET), then formed the Trent Motor Traction Co, Ltd on 1st November, 1913. Trent was jointly owned by BAT and CCHL and took over all six services, the vehicles and the depot at Alfreton, all of which had been developed by CCHL over the previous four years.

The early years of Trent were difficult, as the vehicles were requisitioned by the War Office, but then the Company began to use Tilling-Stevens Petrol Electrics which the Army did not like, and was able to develop its services in a small way around Derby and the surrounding area. In 1915, the Company's presence was established in Uttoxeter New Road, Derby, where it remained until the move to Heanor in 1998.

Two operators were taken over during this time, but the first take-over of any significance was that of Loughborough Road Car Co in February 1919. This expanded the Company's area of operation considerably, and eventually, some 46 operators were taken over from the start until the end of the period covered by the previous volume in 1945.

In 1925 came the first of many SOS vehicles built by the BET associated Midland Red company, and Trent standardised on SOSs until 1937, so that the marque played a major part in the Company's development. Subsequently, many AECs and Daimlers were purchased, as well as further SOSs, followed by utility Daimlers during the war. By about 1935, Trent had largely completed its early development, although in the period 1972 to 1998 there were some significant changes in its operating area, to be described later. At the end of the Second War, there was much to be done in the way of fleet renewal, reinstatement of services suspended during wartime to save fuel, and general adjustment from wartime to peace. It is at that point that this second volume picks up the story.

Six partially new vehicles entered service early in 1946. These were on AEC Regal chassis delivered just as 1945 drew to a close. As described in Part One, six Daimler COG5s with Duple coach bodies had been delivered in 1939. As part of a programme to increase capacity, the bodies were removed from these (and also from nine others with bus bodies) in 1942 and new Willowbrook double deck utility bodies were fitted. The six coach bodies had been stored at Belper Depot, but were refurbished and fitted to the new chassis, with registrations RC 8740-45, but taking the same numbers, 637-42, as the Daimlers. It had also been intended to convert 12 coaches with diesel engines and to reconstruct the bodies, but this proposal was cancelled, and twelve new coaches, AEC Regal IIIs, were ordered instead.

In some ways, it seems odd that coaches should be the first "new" stock after the war. However, as Trent had the spare bodies available, it was sensible to make use of them, and this provided extra vehicles very quickly. As matters turned out, this was fortuitous, because as demand for new bodies built up rapidly, bodybuilders became over-loaded with work and deliveries to the industry generally were often delayed. Also, when the war ended, petrol continued to be in short supply and on ration. Bus operators, however, were able to obtain more fuel, and this enabled them to run excursions and reinstate express services at a fairly early stage. After the long war, with its associated strain and austerity, people were ready to let go and enjoy themselves, and there was increased demand for leisure travel, with more need for coaches than might at first appear. In another vehicle development, those utility double deckers fitted with wartime wooden slatted seats, 1099-1107 and 1301-8, delivered in 1943/4, were converted to upholstered seats, at a cost of £180 per vehicle.

Later in the year, there was new vehicle intake with the arrival of 13 AEC Regent lls with Willowbrook H54R bodies, 1117-29, RC 8915-27, and 34 AEC Regal IIs with Willowbrook B34F bodies, 720-5, RC 8747-52, 726-51, RC 8992-9017. All were fitted with the AEC 7.7 litre diesel engine and crash gearboxes and, along with the coach chassis mentioned earlier, were in fulfillment of an order that had been placed at the turn of 1943/4, during the war. Despite the extensive new vehicle intake, only two vehicles were withdrawn for disposal during 1946, these being two of the 1935 SOS ON coaches with Duple coach bodies. The new vehicles marked the start of a major post war renewal of the fleet, involving both new and refurbished older vehicles. During the period 1946 to 1950 inclusive, no less than 171 completely new vehicles were purchased, all of AEC manufacture, and a refurbishment and rebodying of older vehicles took place which eventually totalled 110 vehicles. By 1950, well over half of the fleet of around 450 vehicles was of modern appearance. Refurbishment of the older vehicles consisted of removal and disposal of the old bodies, and overhaul and refurbishment of the chassis, replacing worn parts, followed by rebodying, mostly by Willowbrook, but with eighteen double deck bodies supplied by Brush. This was after an experimental rebuilding programme involving 1055/71/9 by Willowbrook and 1060, possibly by the Company itself, at the end of 1946.

The first vehicles to be treated were the twelve 1934 SOS ON chassis, 600-11. In 1946, these lost their originally superb Duple Rodney express coach bodies in favour of new Willow brook B35F bodies, being initially renumbered 370-81. Later, in 1949, they were renumbered 500-11, in a new series with some later rebodied SOS DONs. In their new form, effectively as DONs, these vehicles gave a further nine years service, being with-

The first vehicles to be rehabilitated after the war were the twelve SOS ONs of 1934. Their original SOS petrol engines were replaced by new 7.7 litre AEC diesels, already in extensive use in the fleet, which provided improved fuel consumption and power output. The magnificent Duple 34 seat coach bodies were removed and replaced by new Willowbrook B35F bodywork, which was to be the Company's new post-war standard for several years. 508, RC 1808, formerly 378, and originally 608, was photographed in the pub yard at Newark bus station, in the company of one of Lincolnshire Road Car's post-war Bristol Ls with ECW bodywork. The Trent vehicle would have been operating the market day service from East Bridgford, taken over with the business of T A Lewis in 1945.

drawn in 1955. Also in 1946, six of the 1938 Daimler COG5s and four of the 1939 batch received new Willowbrook H54R bodies in place of their previous Weymann front entrance bodywork. They retained the same fleet numbers.

In January 1946 the purchase was formally completed, at a price of £1,300, of a small garage at Castle Donington. Barton had acquired this with their purchase of the business of E & H Frakes, but with the intention of selling the Castle Donington-Derby service, and the garage, on to Trent, retaining the Castle Donington-Long Eaton service themselves. Also in January, the small private hire and excursion business of J Riley of Belper was acquired. No vehicles were involved, but the purchase brought excursions from Belper and Heage,

a football express from Belper to the Baseball Ground at Derby and the private hire book.

Early in 1946, Derby Corporation applied for the "Derby Corporation (Trolley Vehicles) Provisional Order" to authorise (amongst other matters) an extension of their trolleybus route by "six furlongs six chains or thereabouts" along Duffield Road to a point at the junction with Kingscroft, Allestree. At the time, this section was outside the Borough boundary, and the matter was therefore of some concern to Trent. However, negotiations with the Corporation took place, and arrangements made for a joint timetable for Trent buses and Corporation trolleybuses along the route, together with an understanding in relation to any future increases in frequency in Trent services

over the route. Following this, Trent agreed not to object to the Corporation's proposals.

In April 1946, Mr R J Howley, a prominent BET busman who had been a founder Director of the Company, resigned from the Board, of which he was Chairman. Mr R P Beddow, who was a Secretary/Accountant at BET Headquarters, but had at one time been Secretary/Accountant to Trent, took his place. However, Mr J W Womar, also highly experienced, being a former General Manager of the neighbouring North Western Company where he had made an important contribution, was appointed Managing Director and provided the operating experience.

Following their wartime suspension, all the seaside express services were reinstated for the summer 1946. From the June 1946 timetable, the X1 Derby-Manchester, X2 Nottingham-Manchester and the 4, Derby-Buxton services operated jointly with North Western, were also reinstated and, similarly, the middle distance 63 service, Nottingham-Chesterfield, joint with East Midland 12A. Many other wartime suspended services were also reinstated during the course of the year, as part of a continuing, progressive process. A new service was started around the beginning of 1946, this being 106, Belper (Campbell Street)-Ripley via the Isolation Hospital, Nether Heage and Heage.

From June 1946, extra journeys were added to service 68, Nottingham-East Bridgford, which had been acquired the previous year from T A Lewis. The service operated jointly with Skills, who had acquired Jacklin's Elect, of Nottingham. There was also an additional service, 73, Nottingham-Shelford Village, which followed the route of the 68 to Shelford Lane End, and then followed Shelford Lane into the village, there being one journey each way on Monday to Friday evenings. A further new service was 107, Alfreton-Belper (English Sewing Mill), via Somercotes, Leabrooks, Swanwick and Ripley.

Mr Campbell Taylor, who had been General Manager since 1st April 1923 took early retirement from 30th September 1946. It had been his guiding hand that had pursued the Company's development from a still struggling Company with some 40 or so vehicles to one dominating its operating area and running some 450 vehicles throughout Nottinghamshire and Derbyshire, the northern part of Leicestershire and the eastern edge of Staffordshire. The Board recorded their appreciation of his "valuable services" in the Minutes. Mr Campbell-Taylor's retirement was due to ill health, and he moved to Worthing in Sussex to be near the sea air. There he pursued his interest in music but, sadly, died only two or three years later whilst in his late fifties. Mr Campbell- Taylor was succeeded by Mr James Forster, who joined Trent from BET sister company Northern General, which trades today as Go Northern, part of the Go Ahead Group.

1947 opened with appalling, arctic weather, which set in for some three months and was followed by very severe flooding in April. These events led to disruption of services and some lost mileage. Cavendish Bridge, over the River Trent at Shardlow, was destroyed by the flooding, disrupting services to Castle Donington and Loughborough from Derby. The road staff and mechanics put in sterling service and were greatly praised for their efforts in the local press, but many vehicles suffered damage to bodywork, road springs and radiators.

From 5th January, two more services, 124, Loughborough-Wymeswold and Willoughby, and 76, Nottingham-Bulcote serving lightly trafficked rural areas, were reinstated. From 6th January, over 10,000 engineering workers in the area changed from working a 47-hour, five and a half-day week to a 44 hour five day week. This impacted significantly on Trent's operations, for not only did it mean takings on Saturdays were considerably reduced, but also the working day was extended on Mondays to Fridays from 5.30pm to 5.45 pm requiring some extension to spread over duties, which was unpopular with the crews. However, the company was able to resolve this satisfactorily, although Derby Corporation encountered greater difficulty in getting their crews to accept the changes, leading to some initial difficulties. During April, new arrangements

Appalling weather during the early part of 1947 taxed crews severely. The driver of this utility Daimler clears driven snow from his windscreen ready for the journey to Heanor.

were brought into operation for the carriage of parcels between the operating areas of Trent and East Midland using buses of the two companies, and this proved popular with businesses and others.

Another interesting development, during the year, was a change in regulations, which allowed prisoners of war to travel on buses within five miles radius of the camp at which they were stationed. There was some concern about this, however, and the Traffic Commissioners particularly asked operators to let them know of any cases

of strong objections by the public to the presence of prisoners of war on buses, although no great problems seem to have occurred. Under an agreement dated 30th September 1947, the small depot in Argyll Street, Ripley was sold back to the Daley family, from whom it had been acquired with their Pippin Services business in 1935. Although used operationally when initially acquired, it was not used during the war, and it will be recalled from Part One that the depot had been requisitioned by the War Department in 1940, for use as a workshop.

In 1947, it was decided to award long service certificates to those employees with more than twenty five years service, and the first issue of a new "Staff Bulletin & News" was published in February, 1947, to provide information, traffic notices and staff news, being usually published monthly thereafter. From 30th March, later services were reintroduced on many routes, although some of these finished slightly earlier, at around 10.30pm, than they had in pre-war years. At the end of the year Mr R P Beddow resigned from the Board, his place as Chairman being taken by Mr J W Womar, who then resigned his position as Managing Director. During the year, all records in the Company's history had been surpassed, with revenue exceeding £1m, for the first time, and the number of passengers exceeding 55m, with an operated mileage of 1.133m, despite the arctic weather early in the year.

The lost mileage in the early part of the year was made up by the resumption of the seaside express services to Skegness, Great Yarmouth, Blackpool, Scarborough and Cleethorpes, mentioned previously. The tour programme had also resumed, with tours being run to Scotland (7days), Yorkshire Dales and the Lake District (5days) and Wales (5days). These proved extremely popular, but more could not be run, because there was a continuing shortage of suitable hotel accommodation. From 30th March 1947, the previously Sundays only 74, Nottingham-Southwell service was increased to daily, and ticket inter-availability on common sections of route was offered with Mansfield District's service

The first issue of the new Trent Staff Bulletin and News. Printed in black on plain paper, at a size slightly larger than present day A5, the bulletin developed into a regular publication, continuing until 1973. It was later printed on larger and better quality paper and included photographs of people, events and vehicles. Content included the usual new starts, retirements, births, marriages etc, news of company sports fixtures and results (inter-Company matches at cricket and football were a regular part of bus industry life) and enabled the Company to communicate important and useful information to all the staff.

TRENT
MOTOR TRACTION Cº LTD
ASSOCIATED WITH THE BRITISH ELECTRIC TRACTION CO. LTD.
AND THE L.M.S. AND L.N.E. RAILWAYS.

STAFF BULLETIN & NEWS

| FEB. 1947 | FOR STAFF INFORMATION ONLY & NOT FOR PUBLICATION | No. 1 |

FROM THE GENERAL MANAGER'S OFFICE.

A MESSAGE FROM THE GENERAL MANAGER.

It is indeed a pleasure for me to have been given the opportunity of introducing the first issue of the "Trent Staff Bulletin and News."

For some time past the Directors and Management have felt the need for a publication of this sort so that members of the various staffs can be kept informed of the policy and activities of the Company, and how the needs of the public are being met.

At all times the service we give to the public should be the best, and it must be realised that the achievement of this ideal can only be realised by the co-operation and goodwill of every member of the staff. Above all we must act with consideration and courtesy towards the public we serve, bearing in mind that, although most things are in short supply, there need be no shortage of courtesy.

In this, as in subsequent issues of the "Trent Staff Bulletin and News" which will be published at monthly intervals, will be given information of a general character from the General Manager's Office. The Chief Engineer's Department will give information about new vehicles, bodies, garages and equipment, and the Traffic Manager's Department will give news about proposals affecting services and tours.

Sections of the publication will also be devoted to "Public Relations", "Staff" and to various other topics. Individual members of the staff may have interesting news to impart; if so, please don't hesitate to send details to me.

J. FORSTER.

215. The licence for this service had been granted by the Traffic Commissioners, despite opposition from the LMS Railway, but conditional on the loadings being reviewed after three months operation. It was a service, originally running between Oxton, Epperstone and Nottingham, that MDT had acquired from Clarke's of Epperstone and extended to Southwell as a result of the successful licence application. It was not until 1969 that a co-ordinated timetable was introduced on these services, after both operators had been brought under National Bus Company control.

In May 1947, there was an argument in the Traffic Court between Nottingham Corporation on the one hand, and Trent, Barton and Midland General together on the other hand. The Corporation had applied to run from Mount Street Bus Station along Ilkeston Road to Balloon Houses, there turning right along Bilborough Road to Strelley. They argued that Bilborough Road was to be the boundary of a new estate of some 5,000 houses, but were opposed by the three companies, largely on the ground that the Corporation were "staking a claim" and the application was refused by the Commissioners as premature.

More new vehicles arrived during 1947, these being twelve more AEC Regent IIs with Willowbrook H56R bodywork, 1130-41, RC 9646-57, and no less than 43 Regal IIs with Willowbrook B35F bodies, 752-94, RC 9658-700. These vehicles also featured heaters, and similar equipment was retro fitted to the 1946 batch, for which provision to house the equipment had been made by Willowbrook during construction, although the equipment had been unavailable at the time. It will be noted that the double deckers also had an increased seating capacity compared with the previous year's delivery. They were, however, of similar appearance to those delivered in the previous year. There were no existing vehicles refurbished during 1947, but fourteen time expired vehicles were disposed of in March. These included the last two SOS CODs, dating from 1930, seven SOS IM4s dating from 1931-33, and the only one of the 1937 AEC Regent double-deckers not to be rebodied. The AEC later saw service as a cattle float, following removal of the body. Also sold were the last four of the many vehicles acquired from independents during the period of expansion and consolidation in the thirties. These were Dennis Lancets, a marque that found considerable longevity with Trent, the acquired Lancets being concentrated at Loughborough depot. Two of the Lancets had been acquired from Dutton's Unity service of Nottingham, one from C E Salt of Derby and one from R E Horspool of Loughborough.

Although the war had been over since September 1945, men continued to be retained in the Armed Forces. This, together with the continuation of conscription and competition for labour from industry meant that women conductors, who had served the Company so well during the war years, had to be re-engaged in the Company's employment, and this enabled male conductors to be trained as drivers.

On the maintenance side, too, there were difficulties and in first years after the war, staff

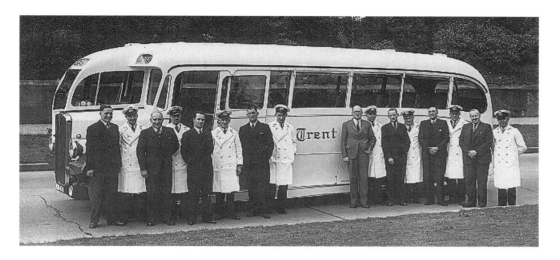

As has been mentioned previously, the Company had a good reputation for its extended holiday tours, and some rather fine looking vehicles for this work arrived in 1948. They were twelve 30 seat Windover bodied coaches on the new AEC Regal III chassis. 600, ACH 430, was taken for an official portrait, along with the team of drivers, in their crisp white dust coats and white topped caps, and guides dressed smartly in lounge suits.

employed were people such as school teachers and anyone with a mechanical bent, willing to try their hand, would be taken on. In particular, fairground showmen were employed to repair vehicles during the winter when the fairgrounds were closed. This led to some incidents that, with hindsight, were quite amusing. For example, bus 1046, one of the pre-war Daimlers, needed a repair to the differential. A showman tried to remove the half shafts, but he burred these to such an extent that the axle had to be removed from the vehicle and sent for repair. Whilst the vehicle stood in Meadow Road depot awaiting return of the axle, the vehicle was cannibalised by the removal of first the engine and then the gearbox. When the axle returned, replacement units had to be found before bus could return to service!

From April 1947, the Company adopted a new livery of BET light red, with ivory window surrounds and roof, to replace the previous overall light red with white roof and BET dark red bands. There had been a brief intermediate stage, from October 1944, in which the livery had been as pre-war, but with the dark red bands omitted.

On 1st January 1948, the railways were nationalised and British Railways was formed under the overall control of the British Transport Commission (BTC), which also had responsibility for the other transport undertakings that were nationalised during this period. The 50% share holding which the LMS and LNE Railways held in Trent therefore fell into state ownership. However, railway directors continued to sit on the Company's Board, and the Standing Joint Committee, set up in 1928 to co-ordinate bus and train journeys, continued to meet. There was little visible change, other than a reference on timetables to services being operated in association with British Railways.

Further AECs arrived in 1948, in the form of twenty AEC Regent lls, 1142-61, ACH 632-51 with Willowbrook H56R bodies and 1320-29, ACH 652-61 with Willowbrook L55R bodies. Also new, for extended tour work, were 600-11,

ACH 430-41, twelve of the new, updated AEC Regal III models with Windover "Huntingdon" C30F coachwork of attractive and stylish appearance. These entered service in May 1948, but were to prove troublesome over the years.

Some forty existing vehicles were overhauled and rebodied during 1948. These were seventeen of the 1937 AEC Regents of the 1015-44 batch, and twenty three Daimler COG5s, eight of 1937, five of 1938, one of 1939 and eight of 1940, all forty of which originally had Weymann front entrance double deck bodies, which were replaced by new rear entrance bodies.

Seven of the AECs received new Willowbrook H56R bodies and were renumbered 1162-8, whilst the remaining ten received new Willowbrook L55R bodies and were renumbered 1330-9. The highbridge vehicles then lasted until 1958, whilst the lowbridge versions were withdrawn in 1959-60. Of the Daimlers, eighteen received new Brush H56R bodies and the remainder new Willowbrook H56R bodies. These vehicles retained their original numbers and lasted until 1957/8, compared with 1954 for the small number retaining their original bodies.

These new and rebodied vehicles enabled some thirty pre-war vehicles to be disposed of. Nineteen IM4s left, together with the remaining 1934 ON coaches and those of 1936, whilst one of the 1936 FEDDs was lost to a fire.

From 10th May 1948, the Standing Passengers Order, 1948 came into force, the effect of which was to allow up to 8 standing passengers on buses, an increase over what had previously been allowed. At the same time, eight "Passengers' Friends" were appointed to operate in Derby Central Bus Station. Dressed in white coats and caps, with armbands marked "Enquiries", their purpose was to answer passengers' questions about bus services. However, this was a development that lasted for only about six months!

During 1948, some 100 Setright Speed ticket machines were taken on hire, and this type of machine eventually replaced the Setright Insert type, although it took some years to cover the whole of the Company's operations. The operation of the Speed machine was similar to the Insert, except that the machine used a continuous paper roll on which it printed the ticket details, rather than the conductor having to insert each ticket separately. After printing, the ticket was torn off against a serrated cutting edge incorporated into the ejection slot.

The resulting tickets, which featured the Company's full title printed continuously along the edge, were rather smaller and had less character than the Insert tickets. However, they saved the conductor from having to carry a rack, and avoided the need for the numbered Insert tickets having to be accounted for, since the number of tickets issued was counted by the machine. The machine was of a horizontally rectangular shape, rather than vertically rectangular, as the previous model, and incorporated an interlock which had to be operated with the left hand, whilst the handle was turned with the right hand. This prevented tickets from being accidentally issued. The conductor received a warning of when the ticket roll was reaching the end, since there was a coloured warning line printed on the centre when sufficient for about fifty tickets remained. The roll could then be changed and the end of the previous roll discarded, usually into the used ticket box.

On 18th June 1948, a new agreement was entered into with Barton for inter-availability of the two Companies tickets on their respective services between Derby and Nottingham. The effect of this was that return tickets bought on one Company's vehicle could be used for return on the other Company's vehicle. This development proved extremely useful, with some 66,000 passengers per month taking advantage of it. The arrangement was later extended to cover the Melbourne-Swadlincote route, and to allow future services to be brought into the agreement, as required. Conductors were required to issue the passenger with an exchange ticket when a ticket of the other Company was presented, and to retain the other Company's ticket to enable revenue to be apportioned. This event marked the start of considerable co-operation with Barton, to the extent that, for many years, the Company

Secretary, Mr E A Yeomans, assisted Barton with hearings in the Traffic Courts, in relation to various licencing hearings. Indeed, when Mr Yeomans retired in 1961, the Barton Directors presented him with a tea trolley, as a mark of respect and appreciation.

1948 as a whole saw all records being broken, with nearly 63million passengers being carried, an increase of 8 million over 1947, which had itself set a record. The seaside holiday services in particular had seen more demand than ever before, to the extent that the Skegness service, which normally operated between Easter and October, was operated at the weekend during the Winter, and a new summer only Skegness service, X11 was started, running from Hucknall via Nottingham. Demand for private hire, excursions and tours also continued to be high, but many passengers had to be disappointed as the Government imposed a 12fi% reduction in fuel for this type of use, and the Company lost revenue, as a result.

Wages to road staff were increasing, in line with those in other industries and with the general increase in the cost of living. They doubled compared with the pre-war figure, although fare levels were the same as those of 1939. The revenue increases due to high demand hid a trend, which was to become of greater significance in future years, when demand for travel began to decline with the advent of television and wider ownership of the private car.

There were further developments of services, and the Allestree services, 56 and 57 were connected to form a circular route, with 56 running out via Kedleston Road, and 57 running out via Duffield Road and Darley Abbey. A new service, 197, ran from Belper (Campbell Street) to Ripley, via Broadholme, Ambergate, Whatstandwell, Crich and Bull Bridge.

In 1949, it was decided to order ten lowbridge deckers and twenty saloons, for 1951 delivery, but it was subsequently decided to defer delivery of these to 1952 at the earliest. In the event, no lowbridge deckers were received until 1956.

The Loughborough-Leicester services, for so long operated jointly with Midland Red, were

renumbered to use the same numbers as that company, as follows: -

121 **Loughborough-Leicester,**
    via Mountsorrel and Red Hill   625

121 **Loughborough-Leicester,**
    via Mountsorrel and Birstall Village 626

121 **Loughborough-Leicester,**
    via Sileby and Rothley House   629

For summer 1949, a new period excursion was introduced from Derby to Rhyl, and this ran on Saturdays from early May to early October, a similar facility being re-introduced between Loughborough and Blackpool, following wartime suspension. The seaside express services continued to experience very heavy demand, although one problem was the practice, common in many industrial areas, of all firms closing down for holidays at the same time, which placed an excessive load on services at that particular time. There were other, more minor service developments, involving additional journeys, as wartime reductions were gradually reinstated, and short workings to East Kirkby on service 61, Nottingham-Mansfield, were renumbered 89. Service 75, Nottingham-Fiskerton was reintroduced and extended to Southwell.

From Sunday 7th August, 1949, following an agreement reached during 1948, new joint services were inaugurated with Derby Corporation serving the Blagreaves Lane and Cavendish areas, on the basis of the revenue of both operators being pooled and apportioned in relation to the existing mileage and revenue returns. The services were 49, Derby, Littleover, Moorway Lane End, Blagreaves Lane End, Sunnyhill, Cavendish, Derby, and 51, following the same route in reverse, together with service 50, Derby-Sunnyhill. These replaced Trent services 49 and 50, Derby-Cavendish, and Corporation service E, Derby-Sunnyhill, which were joined to provide a circular service.

This was considered an event of great moment,

at the time, and was inaugurated by an official event in which a Trent bus ran the route in one direction and a Corporation bus ran in the other, followed by a ceremony at The Council House in Derby. The Chairman, Mr Womar, General Manager, Mr Forster and the other Chief Officials of the Company took part, together with the Council's Deputy Mayor, Chairman of the Omnibus Committee and other Members and Officers of the Corporation. At the same time that these changes came into operation, journeys on service 50, running through to Barrow, were renumbered 23, those on 51, Derby-Uttoxeter, via Denstone, were renumbered 54, and those on 54, Mickleover-Derby, via Havenbaulk Lane, were renumbered 28.

In the course of the ceremonies, Alderman C R Bates of the Corporation mentioned that, during the summer months, many of the Corporation's buses were idle at the weekends, whilst Trent was short of vehicles due to operating additional mileage on excursions and express services. Something, he felt ought to be done about this, and this was, indeed, prophetic, because in due course the Corporation covered all journeys on the joint service on Saturdays, with Trent making up their shortfall of mileage at other times that were less busy for them.

Another area of co-operation at the time was the winter storage of Trent vehicles, surplus to requirements during the winter time, in the Corporation depots at Ascot Drive and Osmaston Road. Several DONs were parked at Ascot Drive, whilst 425 spent at least two years parked in the bus section of Osmaston Road. Others, including 103/4/7/9 and 782 were parked in the trolleybus section at Osmaston Road for one winter. However, when Trent went to collect their vehicles, they were found covered in foundry sand and dirt, having been parked next to the Leys Malleable Castings factory. They all needed a thorough clean and, on removal, hundreds of empty milk bottles were found under and in the vehicles, along with much other rubbish! The practice of parking at these depots ceased shortly after this, although whether there was any connection between the two events is not known.

The negotiations leading to the introduction of the joint operation arose from a loaded question by the Chairman of the Traffic Commissioners, who hinted that he was rather tired of battles between Trent and the Corporation over the Sunny Hill and Blagreaves Lane area. Consequently, the two General Managers, Mr Forster and Mr J E Frith of the Corporation agreed that they would take detailed checks of passenger loadings, total receipts and mileage over a period of several months on their respective services. Using the information obtained from this exercise, they were able to agree on shared services maintaining the ratio arrived at from the checks taken. They also sought in the agreement to safeguard future conditions, such as new housing or other developments, which might lead to modified ratios arrived at after a fair period of time, although, in fact, several years elapsed before any adjustment was found to be necessary.

The joint arrangement proved satisfactory to all concerned. The circumstances were unusual, and great care was taken to meet possible criticism from various parties, by changing over operating duties from time to time to ensure equality of mileage operated. At the time, the fairly elaborate measures taken to ensure that neither side could make any complaint of unfairness, were considered particularly novel.

The success of this joint operation, where previous services of varying characteristics were involved led later to other joint operation with equal sharing of the mileage and receipts. It was soon followed, from October, 1950, by further co-operation, in the form of an agreement to jointly operate a new town service, 14, Tenant Street to Trenton Green, on this basis. This

Willowbrook bodied AEC Regent II 1130, RC9646 of 1948 waits on the stand for the next journey on the Blagreaves Lane (Circular) service, operated jointly with Derby Corporation Omnibus Department from August, 1949. The stand for the service was, in those days, situated rather out of the way in the area reserved for excursions and parking out of service vehicles. The picture was taken sometime during the 1950s.

was to serve Chaddesden Hall, where a new Council housing estate was under development, but where each operator was felt to have a claim on the traffic, although Norman Frost's Felix Bus Service, of Stanley, might also have had a legitimate claim. An earlier development had been the introduction of co-ordinated working on the Coronation Avenue route.

Further records were set up during 1949, when more than 15million miles were run (exceeding 1948 by some 600,000), and 64million passengers carried, but receipts on some 42% of the 74 regular stage carriage services run, did not cover the cost of operation. However, the company accepted these as being part of their obligation as public service vehicle operators to continue to provide the services, so long as the whole operation was economically sound. Perhaps the foreboding of future difficulties were beginning to be felt, however, for the pound was devalued during the year, and this led to an increase of no less than 12½ in the cost of the Company's fuel since this was, of course, all imported. The additional cost resulting from this was £12,500 over a year, but, in addition, national and other pay awards to employees during the year meant that on three occasions during the year, rates of pay for road staff had been increased. Fares had not been generally increased since 1939, but there was concern that, if costs continued to rise, then an increase could not be avoided indefinitely. Equally, there was also recognition that increased fares would mean fewer passengers, resulting in curtailed services.

Some Traffic Commissioners were discussing whether operators should be compelled to give up services, which were not covering their costs. However, there was a remarkable, and indeed, far seeing recognition by the Company of the wider implications of increasing fares in terms of the impact on travellers' pockets, and the increased cost per mile per passenger that would occur if the number of passengers declined. This led to a determination to avoid increases as a contribution towards the production drive, employment and efficiency of the nation.

In May 1949, an inter-hiring agreement was

This newspaper cutting, dated 1948, shows two pre-war AEC Regent chassis undergoing refurbishment in the old Central Works at Great Northern Road, Derby. Discussing the work are Works Manager, Mr C F Dolby, in white coat, and Chief Engineer Mr R C Hunt, both men serving many years with the Company. Mr Dolby began work with Trent in 1924, and was Works Manager from 1948 until retirement in 1968. Mr Hunt joined the Company as Chief Engineer in 1931 remaining in post until retirement in 1958.

concluded with North Western for the loan of vehicles and crews between the two operators at terms to be agreed from time to time. The main purpose of such agreements was to enable drivers of one Company to drive vehicles of the other Company, particularly when working on joint services. This was the first of many such agreements to be concluded over the years.

No new vehicles were received in 1949, but a total of thirty-two vehicles was overhauled and rebodied. These were twelve of the 1937 AEC Regents of the 1015-44 batch, which received new Willowbrook L55R bodies and were renumbered 1340-51, in which form they remained in service until 1958. Also, twenty of the 1936 SOS DONs of the 330-69 batch were overhauled and received

Willowbrook B35F bodies in place of the original Brush bodywork. These were renumbered 512-31 and remained in service until 1958, which compares with 1951-53 for those retaining their original bodies. At the same time, the 1934 SOS ONs, which had been rebodied in 1946 and renumbered 370-81, were renumbered 500-511, to form a complete run.

The influx of rebodied vehicles enabled the last seventeen IM4s to leave the fleet, except for 265, the one that received an experimental Gardner engine in 1933, and which lasted at Wirksworth out-station until 1952, because it was always a good starter. After that, it still eked out a little more life as a service vehicle!

From 1st June 1950, the government increased

the maximum permitted length for vehicles from 26ft (7.925m) to 27ft (8.23m) for double deckers, and from 27ft 6ins (8.382m) to 30ft (9.144m) for single deckers. The Company took advantage of this for all future vehicle orders.

In July, 1950, the Company applied to the Traffic Commissioners to run a service between Mansfield and Derby via Alfreton, but was opposed by Midland General and E Naylor & Sons, both of whom ran between Mansfield and Alfreton, Naylor's following the same route as Trent. This facility had not existed since Trent had abandoned through running in May 1924 but, in addition, they had also briefly run a Derby-Mansfield service via Langley Mill in 1927, doubtless abandoning this in the face of pressure from Midland General. However, in 1950 Midland General and Naylor's objected that they would lose short distance traffic, since passengers wishing to travel to a point south of Alfreton would always use the Trent service rather than choosing from any of three, and changing to the Trent service at Alfreton. The Commissioners refused the application.

It is interesting to note that a count by Trent over a period of several days revealed 830 people transferred travelling north, and 833 people changed travelling south. Only limited thought seems to have been given to the needs of the travelling public, for the Commissioners considered the inconvenience to the public to be "only slight" but also gave considerable weight to the effect of the proposal on competitor services. It was not until after the merger of Trent and Midland General that through running between Mansfield and Derby was established, in 1978.

During 1950, for the first time, there was a decline in the number of passengers carried, which were nearly two million fewer than the previous year. The receipts on stage carriage services were maintained broadly as the previous year, but private hire had fallen noticeably, which was attributed partly to poor summer weather, but also to a decline in people's spending power due to a gradual, but persistent increase in the cost of living.

On a more positive note, the Company's co-ordination policy continued, feeder services from outlying areas being provided in mornings and evenings to railway excursions. Also, through bookings on North Western and PMT services enabled passengers from neighbouring areas to join summer seasonal express services to the east coast resorts served by the company. A scheme for holidays at Blackpool in conjunction with Ribble under the "Easy Way" name also proved popular.

During the year, thirty new AECs were delivered which were of some interest, being ten Regent III models, 1200-9, BRC 400-9 and twenty Regal III models, 100-19, BRC 300-19, all bodied by Willowbrook. A particular feature of the chassis was the use of a Crossley syncromesh gearbox in place of the standard AEC crash box, AEC having taken over Crossley Motors in 1948, and these vehicles were the only AECs so fitted. In addition to these new vehicles, sixteen of the 1937 AEC Regals of the batch 700-19 received chassis overhauls and new Willowbrook B35F bodies, in

which form they lasted in the fleet until 1958, and one, 714, is preserved.

A start was made on disposing of those 1935 SOS DONs that had not been selected for rebodying, ten of these leaving, along with eight of the 1936 SOS FEDDs.

Early in 1950, a new service was introduced, 28D, Derby-Mickleover, via Littleover, Havenbaulk Lane and Staker Lane on Mondays to Saturdays, with three journeys outwards and four inwards. Service 151, Derby-Horsley, was extended to Heanor, via Kilburn, Horsley Woodhouse, Smalley, and Housley Town. From Nottingham, the 68 and 73 services, referred to earlier and serving East Bridgford and Shelford respectively, were improved with more journeys and a fully joint timetable with Skills. There was also a new service, 82, East Bridgford-Bingham, running two journeys daily, with five on Saturday, and a new service, 87, Nottingham-Arnold, via Netherfield, Gedling, Gedling, Mapperley Plains and Beechwood Avenue.

Many people would say "a brand new bus", and certainly few would recognise any difference. Only the shallow pre-war radiator, and the registration number tell those with sufficient knowledge that the chassis of this vehicle has already put in many years of service. 1349, RC 4645, a 1937 AEC Regent was photographed at Nottingham's Granby Street in 1951, two or three years after receiving its new lowbridge Willowbrook body.

This busy scene at Nottingham Huntingdon Street in June 1955, shows 1245, DRC 945, one of the Leyland bodied PD2s delivered towards the end of the period covered by this Chapter. The opening vents on the front upper deck windows were unique to this vehicle, having been offered to the Company as a trial. They had a remarkable effect on the appearance.

Chapter Two
Last of the Golden Years
1951-53

A draconian increase in fuel tax in 1951, from 9d (3.75p) to 1/6d (7.5p), together with increases in the costs of stores, materials, spare parts and wages led the company to make its first application for a general, albeit modest, increase in fares, despite earlier determination to avoid this. This was put into effect from 20th June, 1951, but, before the case came before the Traffic Commissioners for hearing, the Chancellor of the Exchequer had increased fuel tax by a further 4½ (1.875p). This could not be taken account of in that first application, and nor could changes in the cost of the fuel itself, also increased, or further wage increases for road and maintenance staff. These led to total increases in costs of some £65,000, and a second fares increase had to be sought. However, the year saw some improved weather, and the Company's passenger carryings increased by 2 million to their former levels.

One particular area of concern, then, as now, was peak hour travel, and the fact that more than 45% of the Company's fleet was required solely to cater for peak workers travel, being needed for less than 4 hours per day. The need to provide these vehicles at fares well below normal meant that, almost by definition, workers traffic was unremunerative, and the Company complained that it was time that workers fares were done away with.

Further extended through bookings were developed during the year to enable North Western passengers from Manchester to travel through to the East Anglian coast, and an innovative stay at home holiday was developed. Introduced as a cheaper alternative to the extended tour, these were entitled "Five Ways in Five Days", comprising a tour with meals provided to a different place each day, returning home in the evening. This development proved very popular, especially from

the main traffic centres of Derby and Nottingham.

A typical example of the programme for this type of holiday was: Monday to North Wales, Tuesday to the Peak District, Wednesday to Sandringham and Hunstanton, Thursday to Alton Towers, and Friday to the Wye Valley and the Malvern Hills.

A further period excursion was started in 1951, running between Nottingham and Hunstanton, and a new seasonal service from Hucknall was the 140 to Gunthorpe, running via Broomhill, Arnold, Beechwood Road, Mapperley Plains, Gedling, Burton Joyce and Lowdham. This was a Sundays only two hourly service starting at 11.00am, to serve what we now regard as the leisure market, Gunthorpe Bridge, on the River Trent, being a noted picnic spot.

At Derby, new services introduced were a Friday and Saturday service 26, Derby-Stenson, via Blagreaves Lane End, and a Fridays only circular service 153, Derby-Hollington, via Mackworth, Kirk Langley, Brailsford, Ruck of Stones, Ednaston, Hollington, Long Lane, Osliston Lane End, Dalbury Hollow, Radbourne Common and Markeaton Lane. This replaced previous services 153, Derby-Trussley and Church Broughton, and 156, Derby-Hollington, via a different route.

Building works took place at Meadow Road depot, where the extension constructed during the war to house gas producer trailers was converted to a paint shop able to accommodate six vehicles, compared with three vehicles that could be accommodated at the old paint shop at Central Works. This new facility enabled all vehicles to receive a repaint or revarnish at an average of every fifteen months, compared with the previous average of every thirty months.

Also during 1951, in June, a start was made on extending Belper depot, which the Company had previously started during the war, but been forced to abandon due to difficulty in obtaining materials.

The newly completed paint shop, opened at Meadow Road depot in 1951, using the part of the building constructed to house gas producer units during the war years.

This action shot, taken by Geoff Atkins at Sherwood in March 1951 when the vehicle had just been delivered, shows one of the first new Leyland double deckers to be bought by the Company. Indeed, they were almost certainly the first Leyland double deckers to be owned. 1221, CCH 621, was one of a batch of six Leyland PD2/3s, with Leyland H56R bodywork developed from a design of 1936-8.

The Company's co-ordination efforts continued, with interavailability of road/rail tickets extended to the Derby-Nottingham, Derby-Burton, Derby-Manchester and Nottingham-Manchester services.

During 1951, the Company received its first ever bulk delivery of new Leylands, 1220-25, CCH 620-5, which were Leyland Titan PD2/3s, with Leyland H56R bodies. They enabled the last six of the 1936 SOS FEDDs to be withdrawn, some of this batch having covered more than half a million miles during their fifteen year service life. As a result, they were in very poor condition, being said by staff to be held together with "string and wire", to keep them going. A further nine DONs were also sold, at the same time.

Ten Leyland Royal Tiger coaches with Leyland C41C coachwork of restrained but well proportioned appearance were also received during 1951, but no coaches were withdrawn as a result of these arrivals

During the early part of 1952, the Traffic Commissioners granted the Company's second blanket application for a fares increase. Here it is possible to see the start of the developing trend of regular fares increases, brought about by increasing costs and declining traffic, and this was to become a feature of bus operations over the next two or three decades, having a damaging effect on the industry generally. However, whereas fuel tax had been 9d (3.75p) per gallon at the end of the war, it had reached 2/6d (12½) by 1952. This,

coupled with increasing wages, not only in the face of inflationary pressures, but also to combat a severe staff shortage as people sought work with more congenial working hours, meant that fares increases were more or less inevitable. In an effort to minimise the impact, however, it also led Trent, as other companies, to seek economies in various forms. The fuel tax also led to the appearance in the Company's vehicles of posters protesting at the level of fuel tax which bus companies had to bear.

In order to increase the Company's working capital, reserves of £337,680 were capitalised by a rights issue of new shares at a rate of 5 new for every 8 existing shares held, to increase the issued stock to £877,968. Despite the increased fares, the number of passengers carried, and the mileage operated continued to show a slight increase. However, in common with the rest of the industry, the increase in traffic was beginning to level, as people bought televisions and stopped using the bus to go to the cinema. They also bought cars, or received lifts in cars, which reduced their reliance on buses.

There were service developments in 1952, however and from Derby, a new service was 155, to Markeaton Park, via Chain Lane, Western Road, Mickleover Station, and Radbourne Lane, which used the number 156 for journeys in the reverse direction, these journeys replacing service 16 to Mickleover Station. Service 26, Derby-Stenson was extended via Twyford to Barrow. On express services, one journey on service X7, Nottingham-Great Yarmouth, was extended to start at Derby, and service X13, Nottingham-Sandringham and Hunstanton replaced the period excursion from Nottingham to Hunstanton. A new period excursion was introduced on Saturdays from Loughborough to Great Yarmouth.

New vehicles acquired during 1952 were further Leylands in the form of ten PD2/12s with longer Leyland H56R bodies, 1226-35, CRC 826-35, and ten Royal Tiger single deckers with Leyland B41F bodies, 800-9, DCH 900-9. The twenty new buses enabled a further eighteen pre-war SOS DONs to go, and also sold was the last of a batch of 1926 SOS FSs acquired second hand from Midland Red in 1935. It had been converted to dual controls, for use as a driver tuition bus, when the others had been sold in 1937.

During the early fifties the Derby War Memorial Village was under development at Shelton Lock, to provide homes for those severely wounded in the war. The Company donated a bungalow, under a seven year endowment scheme, whilst Trent employees made donations towards the upkeep of the estate by deductions from their pay. The property was occupied by an ex service-man who had lost the lower part of his legs, and his family.

An interesting development, begun in Summer 1953, was a through booking to the Isle of Man using air travel between Blackpool Airport and Ronaldsway Airport, Isle of Man, at an inclusive fare of £5. This utilised the service of the Lancashire Aircraft Corporation Ltd, flying a de Haviland Dragon Rapide aircraft. On Saturdays, a Trent coach ran direct to Blackpool, but during the week passengers used the X1 Derby-Manchester service, changing at Manchester onto a Blackpool service run jointly by Ribble and North Western.

The third blanket fares increase took place in March 1953 and, together with that which had

taken place in April 1952 resulted in increased receipts, which helped to offset the seemingly ever rising costs. However, there was also increased business on private hire, day excursions and extended tours, which helped offset the losses incurred on rural and workers services. There were also efforts to reduce costs by new methods and in particular a change to lower viscosity engine oil was useful in reducing fuel consumption.

Further expansion took place during 1953 including, in September, the take over of the business of Allen's Motor Services of Mountsorrel, bringing additional Loughborough Town Services, two of which had previously been joint with Allen's since take over from R E Horspool in 1935.

Added to this were further holiday tours, which attracted record numbers of travellers, and a new Saturdays express service, X14, Mansfield-Great Yarmouth, via East Kirkby, Hucknall, Nottingham and then via the X7 route. Also, the Manchester services from Derby and Nottingham were extend-ed through to Blackpool on Ribble, North Western and Lancashire United licences using "On Hire" and "For Blackpool " labels affixed to the wind-screen to enable through running over sections for which Trent did not have a licence.

Two new stage carriage services were introduced during the early part of the year. On Sundays, Thursdays and Saturdays only, service 65A started, running between Nottingham and Clifton, serving Wilford Hill Cemetery, Ruddington Hospital and Ruddington Station, and also service 65B, Nottingham-Bunny, via West Bridgford, Wilford Hill Cemetery, Ruddington Village and Bradmore Lane End, but running on a daily basis. Also, a further Sundays only service started to Gunthorpe, 141 from Bilborough, via Bells Lane, Hucknall Road, then following the line of the 140 route, via Arnold, Mapperley Plains, Gedling, Burton Joyce and Lowdham.

In the autumn 1953, many services were renumbered, using letter suffixes, as shown by the list in the Appendix.

Vehicle deliveries for 1953 were a further fifteen PD2/12s with Leyland H56RD bodies, 1236-50, DRC 936-50, which were the first double deckers to feature power doors, and also a further six Royal Tiger coaches. This time the coaches were fitted with Willowbrook C41C bodywork to a rather more flamboyant style than those supplied by Leyland two years previously.

The PD2s enabled the withdrawal of the 15 1938 Daimler COG5/40s that had been rebodied with double deck utility bodies during the war - the first buses in the fleet with utility bodies to be withdrawn. The cooling capacity of these vehicles as double deckers sometimes proved inadequate, and they were quite prone to boiling, commonly being referred to by drivers as "kettles"! Also sold were an assortment of other pre war vehicles that had been left out of the post war rebuilding programme - a 1938 Daimler COG5 double decker, three of the four pre-war AEC Regals and the last twelve remaining SOS DONs that had retained their original bodies were stripped of usable spares and disposed of.

With an eye to future development of the Company's Derby facilities, five cottages, nos. 11, 13, 14, 15 and 16 Great Northern Road; and three houses, nos. 44, 46 and 50 Uttoxeter New Road were purchased, but the redevelopments were to wait many years before they could take place.

This de Haviland Dragon Rapide aircraft of the Lancashire Aircraft Corporation was used by Trent passengers on the coach-air service to the Isle of Man, inaugurated during the summer, 1953.

During the period covered by this Chapter, lighter weight vehicles entered the fleet. One of these, a Saro bodied Leyland Tiger Cub, 812, FCH 12, delivered in 1954 and allocated to Hucknall depot at the time, leaves Mount Street Bus Station in Nottingham for Hucknall's Beauvale Estate, on service 60B. This variant of service 60, together with service 60A serving Ruffs Estate, was introduced in 1955.

Chapter Three
Cutting Costs
1954-57

In January, 1954, an interhiring agreement was concluded with Ribble (this was later to be extended, in October 1962, to include the vehicles of the latter's subsidiary companies Standerwick and Scout), and this was followed in April by a similar agreement with East Midland.

Also during 1954, the small garage at Castle Donington, acquired from E & H Frakes, via Barton Transport in 1946 ceased to be used and was sold. There was a dispute with Derby Corporation over their proposals to extend trolley bus services to Breadsall, which the Company opposed and which became the subject of a Public Inquiry. Also a further dispute was about proposals to increase the departure charges from Derby bus station which was, eventually withdrawn.

Two new services were started during 1954, these being 10, Derby-Kirk Hallam, started in February, and intended particularly to serve a large new housing estate, and 44, Derby-Chesterfield started in August jointly with East Midland and Midland General, a development which was particularly interesting.

Readers of Part One will recall that in 1931 Trent and East Midland applied for a licence to run between Derby and Chesterfield, but this was turned down due to strong objection by the LMS Railway. There matters rested for many years, but a key event was the take-over by East Midland of the independent operator A Heeley of New Tupton, who had a licence to run between Chesterfield and Clay Cross.

Midland General held a licence for their service D2, Alfreton-Clay Cross, whilst Trent, of course, had their service 1, Derby-Alfreton, long established since the Commercial Car Hirers days. This meant that the three operators covered the whole line of route and a new application for a licence was lodged which, despite opposition

from Chesterfield Corporation, was granted, a new hourly service starting on 29th August 1954, the three operators running a journey in turn.

As is well known, Midland General used a system of route numbers with a letter prefix, introduced by Douglas Hays in 1936. During the planning of the new service, it had been intended to number it 01, on the ground that 0 could be taken as either a letter or a number and therefore suited all three operators' systems. Correspondence about this took place between Uttoxeter New Road and Langley Mill, reaching agreement, but then East Midland objected, because they used a fare stage numbered 01 and, they said, conductors might be confused. So the service was given the much more ordinary number 44, instead!

The 155/6, Derby-Markeaton Park services, started in 1952, proved to be short-lived, as these reverted to a Derby-Mickleover service, numbered 15B in 1954. However, express services were the subject of further development, with the following additions, running on summer Saturdays only:

X15 **Nottingham-Lowestoft,**
    via Radcliffe, Bingham, Grantham,
    Great Yarmouth, Gorleston and Hopton.
X16 **Hucknall-Cleethorpes,**
    via East Kirkby and Mansfield
X23 **Manchester-Skegness,**
    via Stockport, New Mills, Buxton,
    Bakewell, Matlock, Ambergate,
    Nottingham, Newark, Lincoln, Wragby,
    Horncastle and Burgh.
    Jointly operated with North Western.

From Nottingham, a new service, 77, ran two journeys per day to Gedling, via Carlton, starting from the City's Mount Street Bus Station, but also serving that at Huntingdon Street.

The fourth fares increase was implemented from 22nd August 1954. Mention has been made of the increasing costs faced by the Company since the war. This was particularly in the cost of fuel and, in an effort to combat this the industry was turning to lighter weight vehicles. Leyland had introduced their Tiger Cub PSUC1/1 chassis

in 1952, and the BET Group had placed an initial bulk order for 500 for distribution amongst its subsidiary companies. Trent received twenty Tiger Cubs, 810-29, FCH 10-29, the first ten having B44F bodywork by Saro (Saunders Roe Engineering and Shipbuilding Co, of Anglesey), and the second ten, 820-9, FCH 20-9, had B44F bodies by Weymann.

The arrival of these twenty buses enabled the 1939/40 SOS SON buses and coaches to be withdrawn, along with a number of pre-war vehicles, a total of thirty seven vehicles being disposed of. Also delivered towards the end of 1954 was 120, GCH 120, a further Tiger Cub but fitted with a Willowbrook DP41F body, which was the prototype of a batch of ten and had been exhibited at the Commercial Motor Show at Earls Court.

The Tiger Cub chassis was equipped with an electrically operated Eaton two speed axle. This gave cruising advantages, and was excellent when drivers had mastered the technique for its use, but could be difficult to use and become troublesome. The vehicles were very suitable for use on express services in those pre Motorway times, but could also be used on stage carriage services.

During the year, Mr S Ferry, Traffic Manager since the twenties, was awarded the MBE, and at the end of the year, Mr J Forster, General Manager left to take up a similar post with his former company, Northern General. He was replaced by Mr W Leese, previously with neighbouring East Midland.

The trolleybus extensions proposed by Derby Corporation, referred to earlier, were subject to a Public Inquiry and the Minister of Transport determined that he was not prepared to proceed with the proposed Order. However, during the negotiations, the Corporation agreed to withdraw that part of their proposals for a trolley service to Breadsall following an agreement with Trent for a joint service, which in due course materialised as service 27, Bus Station-Scarborough Rise.

The rise in costs, accompanied by a spiral of rising fares continued, and the Company implemented its fifth fares increase from 24th April, 1955, following the agreement of the Traffic

The prototype dual purpose bodied Leyland Tiger Cub, 120, GCH 120 appeared on the Willowbrook stand at the 1954 Commercial Motor Show at Earl's Court, as shown here. This particular vehicle served the Company well, remaining in service for some fifteen years, a considerable period for an essentially lightweight vehicle. Note the relatively small diameter of the wheels, and the attractive livery style, including the fleetname, enclosed in bright metal moulding, making the vehicle instantly recognisable as a "semi-coach" to use the Company's term.

Commissioners to their application.

A reserve was placed with Leyland Motors Ltd for 44 double deck chassis for delivery in 1958, and these were to prove interesting, when they arrived, but more immediately the new deliveries for 1955 were a further six PD2/12s with Leyland H56RD bodies, 1251-6, FRC 951-6. They were similar to those delivered in 1953, but of particular interest as they were the last bodies to be built by Leyland at their Farington works at Leyland, the bodyshop concentrating on the production of truck cabs thereafter. The final one, 1256, is preserved following a few years post Trent service with Whippet of Fenstanton and, at the time of

writing, is at the Wythall Museum of the Birmingham and Midland Motor Omnibus Trust (BaMMOT).

The balance of the Willowbrook dual purpose Tiger Cubs, foreshadowed by 120, were received, 121-9, GRC 121-9, but there were also a further ten with Weymann bodies, 130-9, GRC 130-9. The Weymann bodied vehicles were of identical concept to the Willowbrook bodied examples, but the bodies were based on the same shell as buses 820-9. The front was suitably modified, with a flush windscreen, making it a little less bus-like, and there was a two piece rear window at the back, with the emergency exit moved from the back to

the middle of the off side. These were followed, later in the year by a further twelve Willowbrook examples, 140-151, HRC 140-151.

Also new during the year were six Tiger Cub coaches for extended tour work, 216-21, GRC 216-21, which had Burlingham centre entrance 41-seat bodywork to the classic Seagull design. As a result of these new arrivals, the last remaining SOSs were withdrawn, ending a thirty years period of operation of the marque that had done so much to progress the Company's early development.

With effect from 31st July 1955, the Belper-Shottle service of H S North Transport was taken over. It was extended to Cross o' th' Hands, via Turnditch and numbered 92. Readers of Part One will recall that North had previously been taken over by Trent in 1935. However, he had subsequently taken over the Shottle service from P W Poundall in 1936, and had then made good business on contract work during the war years. He continued with this and private hire work after selling the Shottle service to Trent, finally selling this part of the business to another firm, which closed the operation fairly soon afterwards.

During the course of the year, Midland Red had purchased the businesses of Kemp and Shaw, a company associated with Allen's of Mountsorrel, operating between Leicester, Loughborough and Derby, and also the remaining service of Allen's itself, operating between Loughborough and Leicester. It was agreed that Trent should take a share of the increased business between Loughborough and Leicester and also the whole of the increased service between Loughborough and Derby.

The apportionment was agreed on a mileage basis, and Trent paid Midland Red £6660 for the Leicester-Loughborough section, and £3838 for the Loughborough-Derby portion. However, Midland Red continued as service X63 the ex Kemp and Shaw service running Leicester-Loughborough-Derby until 1961, when there was a further rationalisation.

Further service expansion led to the introduction of new summer express services for the 1955 season, as shown in the list below:

X13, **Alfreton-Great Yarmouth,**
via Ripley, Heanor and Ilkeston.
Operated jointly with Midland General.

X17, **Loughborough-Great Yarmouth**
via Kings Lynn and Norwich.

X18, **Loughborough-Blackpool,**
via Derby, Ashbourne, Macclesfield,
Winwick and Wigan.

X19, **Derby, Nottingham-Clacton on Sea**,
via Melton Mowbray, and Colchester.
Operated jointly with Barton.

X20, **Nottingham-Cromer,**
also serving Hunstanton, Brancaster,
Wells next the Sea, Blakeney,
Sheringham and West Runton.

The X17/8 services both replaced previously operated period excursions, and the X20 saved passengers the inconvenience of changing onto local stage carriage services for these resorts when using the Thursdays and Sundays X13 Nottingham-Hunstanton service. The X13 was renumbered X21, to allow the previous number to be used for the new Great Yarmouth service, as it was the next number in joint operator Midland General's series. In addition to these new services, a new period excursion was introduced between Barrow on Soar and Skegness.

A new service to serve Bretby Hospital on visiting days at the children's' hospital, was 5H, via Havenbaulk Lane, Willington, Repton, Newton Solney and Burton. The Ockbrook and Borrowash services were recast with revised numbers, and alternate journeys on the Allestree services were diverted via West Bank Road and Woodlands Road, to serve Woodlands Estate using numbers 56A and 57A.

Daily services introduced to serve newly built estates at Hucknall were 60A, and 60B following the 60 route to Hucknall Market Place and then terminating at Ruffs Estate or Beauvale Estate respectively. At Ripley, there was a new daily service, 102, from Ripley Market Place to Ash Crescent/Pear Tree Avenue.

In 1956, Midland General proposed new Mansfield-Torquay and Mansfield-Bournemouth seasonal weekend express services, possibly as a result of their success with the recently introduced seasonal express operation to Great Yarmouth, which was operated jointly with Trent. A difficulty was that the new proposals potentially interfered with some established operations, including both the Associated Motorways and Yorkshire Services pools, but it was decided to go ahead regardless of this.

The Associated Motorways pool was indeed deeply disturbed by the proposal and their management committee invited Midland General to a meeting to discuss the matter. At that meeting, it was clearly stated that any service duplicating the existing services from Derby and Nottingham through Cheltenham to the south coast would be vigourously opposed. The Associated Motorways management committee strongly considered that any newly identified need should be met by exten-sions of their existing Derby and/or Nottingham services on a daily basis. They were also firmly of the view that "creaming off" full loads at peak periods, which is what the Midland General proposal to operate only at weekends during the main holiday season amounted to, was unacceptable.

The management committee felt that the correct way of providing for the newly identified demand was by of an extension of their Nottingham service to Mansfield and possibly the Derby service as well (but by different routes) on both day and night journeys. Trent and Midland General were offered participation in these proposals in the form of hiring their vehicles to Associated Motorways for through operation to Torquay and Bournemouth. Full agency control of

One of the final batch of Leyland bodied PD2s, 745, FRC 955, scurries along Derby's Morledge in the mid-day sun, as the conductor resets the three track route number blind from the upper deck. The picture was taken in the early sixties, by which time the vehicle had been renumbered from 1255. In the background, one of Barton's noted BTD2 rebuilds, with Northern Counties body, begins the return journey to Nottingham.

the new area was also offered, Trent, of course, having already acted for many years as control agents for Associated Motorways in the Derby and Nottingham areas. Application for the extension of the Nottingham service to Mansfield was made by the pool in October 1956 and was granted in the Western and East Midland Traffic Areas, and although Trent curiously entered a formal objection, they made no appearance at the hearings before the Traffic Commissioners. Subsequently, the management committee agreed that Trent and Midland General jointly should apply for a new service to Cheltenham (with a qualified picking up area) and if the service proved successful they would bring it into the Pool, with the Mansfield extension already granted to Associated Motorways then being withdrawn. In due course, this application was made, by Trent and Midland General, but subsequently withdrawn and the Associated Motorways Nottingham-Mansfield extension was allowed to stand, whilst the extension by Associated Motorways of their Derby service to Mansfield was never pursued.

Although the Associated Motorways management committee were prepared to consider this participation by Trent and Midland General with Associated Motorways, this would have been on the basis of a mileage based hiring rate or eventual membership at the "pool" rate. Both of these were well below the revenue that could be expected from independent summer weekend working, and doubtless did not have the same appeal. However, having realised that any further unilateral action would result in "strong opposition," together with the fact that Associated Motorways had now secured a foothold in Mansfield by extension of their Nottingham service, the two companies concluded that there was little chance of success and they withdrew the proposals. Whilst Trent might have benefited from these Torquay/Bournemouth proposals, Midland General were the instigators of them and Trent's involvement did not show any great enthusiasm.

However, an interhiring agreement with Midland General was concluded in May 1956, doubtless to help with the X13 Alfreton-Great Yarmouth service, started the previous year, and any further express developments.

Once again, the Company implemented a further fares increase, its sixth, from 14th February, 1956 but, at the same time, operating costs reached an all time high during the year, and there remained continual pressure on costs. Indeed, a large number of services, 47% of those operated, 25% of the mileage, continued to be run at a loss.

In March, the former Peel Foundry, adjacent to Meadow Road depot, was purchased, with the intention of extending the depot - accommodation had become inadequate as vehicle sizes increased.

On 7th July 1956, the business of E Naylor & Sons, of South Normanton was acquired with nine vehicles, and a stage carriage service operating between Alfreton and Mansfield via Fulwood and Sutton in Ashfield. In this corridor, Trent already had a service, 100, over the same route, into which the former Naylor journeys were incorporated. Midland General were also active with their route C2, Alfreton-Mansfield via South Normanton, Pinxton, Kirkby in Ashfield and Sutton in Ashfield, acquired with the business of Pinxton Bus Co in February, 1935. Trent had first been invited by Naylor's to make an offer in April, 1956, but Naylor's then went into negotiations

Naylor's had a fairly modern, if varied, fleet of vehicles, painted in a red and cream livery that gave them a "large operator" appearance. However, an elderly vehicle was this 1932 AEC Regent, VO 8566, which had once been 66 in the Mansfield District fleet, when it had a Weymann H54R body. Withdrawn by MDT in 1946, it was sold to Naylor's who had it rebodied by Burlingham, as shown, in 1949. The vehicle was photographed at Alfreton, immediately after the sale, when the Trent number plate, 1218, with yellow background for allocation to Alfreton depot, had been fitted, but before repainting into the Company's livery. Despite its age, and unpopularity with drivers, it remained with Trent until 1959.

with Midland General, and continued to do so for some three months, finally seeming to agree a price. However, Naylor's then went back to Trent and agreed to sell to them. Not unnaturally, Midland General were most unhappy about this. However, the price offered by Midland General was presumably less than that offered by Trent, whose price paid was certainly no higher than that which the Board had originally authorised to be offered when they first considered the matter in February. However, Midland General also felt that their service was of equal standing to the Trent one, and that there should be an equal merger between the two, which they had sought to negotiate for a number of years. Trent, however, were unwilling to negotiate, and, it is said, wanted to buy Naylor's in order to negotiate with Midland General from a position of greater strength.

From the Midland General side, the wish to acquire Naylor's was said to be to influence Trent's attitude to negotiations, since Naylor's service was in less direct competition with their service than it had been with Trent's. In fact, such a merger of the services did, eventually, take place, but not until both companies became state owned from 1969. Then, the services were rationalised and operated by the two Companies on a joint basis, but a Midland General viewpoint on this was that they had acquired half of the total service, but without paying out to buy Naylor's!

During 1956, a start was made on a full conversion to Setright Speed ticket machines in replacement of the previous Insert models, an order being placed for 600 machines, followed by 300 in 1957 and 300 in 1958. This followed the 100 such machines taken on hire in 1948.

From the May 1956 timetable, through journeys to Blackpool were shown as jointly operated by Trent, North Western, Ribble and the original, Atherton based independent, Lancashire United. These ran via the X2 route from Nottingham to Manchester, and thereafter via Chorley and Preston over the line of the Ribble/North Western/LUT X60 and X70 service. The licence for this pair of services had a generous duplication allowance, and it was once known as

the busiest express bus service in the country.

Trent vehicles on these journeys carried "On Hire to North Western" windscreen stickers over the Manchester-Blackpool section. Similar arrangements applied in respect of the X1 route from Derby via Ashbourne. So far as is known, few, if any, LUT vehicles ventured south of Manchester on this service. Appearances by Ribble vehicles in that area were also limited, although, for a time, a Ribble vehicle on layover in Nottingham operated a journey on Trent's East Bridgford-Newark service on summer Saturdays.

Often, the vehicles used by North Western and Ribble, some of which would overnight at a Derby depot , were older types. However, it was often a case of pressing into service whatever was available, and Trent, for its part, would also supply odd

vehicles, such as Royal Tiger and Tiger Cub buses. The rear two double seats would be removed from these, to provide space for luggage, with the seats being replaced ready for normal service on Monday, this being a regular practice during this period.

The Trent timetable additionally indicated onward connections to Liverpool, Preston, Lancaster, Kendal and Keswick, using Ribble services X10, X20, X30 and X40. On Saturdays only, one journey ran each way between Nottingham and Liverpool, and other connections were also shown using Ribble X50, Manchester-Morecambe, and X27 and 100, Preston-Southport. Connections for Glasgow and Edinburgh using Ribble services were also shown. Also for 1956, the Derby-Rhyl period excursion, established from

It was always a problem to find sufficient vehicles on a summer Saturday when there were express services to be covered. Ribble was a joint operator on the X2 service in respect of through journeys to and from Blackpool and, as a result, regularly had a vehicle on layover in Nottingham on summer Saturdays. Trent took advantage of this and used it on the 81, East Bridgford-Newark service. Note the "On Hire to Trent" sticker in the windscreen of Ribble 921, FCK 421, a Leyland bodied Royal Tiger, of 1953, entering rural Kneeton.

1949, was extended back to Belper, Ripley and Alfreton.

Property developments continued, and land was bought at Ashbourne, Loughborough and Belper to enable depot improvements to take place in due course.

Further consideration was given to future vehicle orders, and the option previously taken out for Leyland double deckers was finned up as 22 Titan PD3/4s and 22 of the new Atlantean chassis, subject to satisfactory service trials of the latter. Both these developments were of interest. From 1st July 1956, the regulations on the length of double deck vehicles had been amended to permit lengths up to 30ft (9.144m), and the PD3 was Leyland's response to this, being essentially an extended PD2 with slightly uprated components where made necessary by the additional weight.

The Atlantean chassis had been under development for some time as the Lowloader, a rear engine, rear entrance vehicle with the front axle in the then conventional position. However, it was shown in what turned out to be its ultimate layout, with front entrance, set back front axle and rear engine at the 1956 Commercial Motor Show, but was to be subject of considerable further development. It was to be 1959/60 before Trent's order materialised in slightly different form, but the PD3s were delivered in 1958.

In the meantime, new vehicles delivered in 1956 were further Leyland PD2/12s, 1257-66, JCH 257- 6, and 1352-7, JCH 352-7. The chassis were much as delivered in previous years but, as mentioned previously, Leyland had ceased bus body building and these vehicles were bodied by Metro- Cammell, to their Orion design, 1256-65 being H58RD bodies, and 1352-7 being lowbridge L55RD bodies. Mention has been made of the continuing cost pressures, and the Orion was a lightweight design, intended to reduce fuel consumption. These vehicles enabled a start to be made on withdrawal of the utility Daimlers, and also one or two of the rebodied pre-war Daimlers left the fleet. The six 1946 AEC Regals with pre-war coach bodies were also withdrawn.

At the close of the year, from 17th December,

1956, fuel rationing, not seen since the years after the war, was again introduced. This was due to the Suez crisis, a result of which was that oil tankers from the Middle East were unable to use the Suez canal and had to travel instead by the much longer sea route via the Cape of Good Hope, on the southern tip of Africa. Mileage had to be reduced, but peak facilities maintained, and although the event led to a temporary increase in passenger numbers, this turned out to be artificial, beginning to fall away long before the crisis was over. Associated with the crisis, the government imposed a fuel duty surcharge, and allowed operators to surcharge fares by ½d (0.21p) on fares between 2½d (1.04p) and 8½d (3.54p) and 1d (0.42p) on fares over 9d (3.75p). This continued until 24th April 1957, when the fuel duty surcharge was removed.

The by now regular fares increase took place in February 1957, and a further increase, the eighth, was implemented the following September. These,

together with a strike by road staff during July, a peak period of the year, encouraged the continuing fall in passenger numbers, which was particularly marked during the course of the year.

In common with other major operators (although locally, major independent Barton was not affected, and continued to run alongside the small independents Felix, and Blue Bus services), the Company experienced an all out strike over wages, lasting from 20th to 28th July, 1957. During this time, no services ran, losing a total of fi million miles and costing some £60,000 in lost revenue. This strike followed a wages claim that the Trade Unions had lodged in the Spring for a substantial increase. Agreement could not be reached, and as the Unions refused to go to arbitration, the employers eventually imposed an increase of 3/- (15p) per week. The Unions objected to the increase being granted without their agreement and called a full-scale national strike. This was settled with an increase of 11/- (55p) per

Following the end of bodybuilding at Leyland, the new supplier, Metro-Cammell, produced a lightweight body of very different, and somewhat austere style, although the general outline was not unattractive, and the chassis was the by now familiar Leyland Titan PD2/12. 1012, KCH 112, of the second batch delivered in 1957, was caught by the camera operating a journey on the X42 Derby-Nottingham express service, doubtless one Saturday when the normal dual-purpose single decker was doing an express journey to the seaside. It appears about to be overtaken by a Ford 100E car, a model not noted for its sparkling performance!

week being paid from 29th July, this being inclusive of the 3/- already granted.

Trent has generally enjoyed good labour relations down the years, and major strike action by bus staffs has been remarkably rare over many years, even during the period of continuing national industrial unrest of the late nineteen seventies. However, at this time, workers were under pressure from a constantly rising cost of living, and bus companies were under the twin pressures of rising costs and falling traffic. These factors would doubtless have contributed to the frustration leading to large-scale action, largely out of the character of the work force involved. However, the results were unfortunate for, during the period of the strike, people had to find alternative ways of travelling, and many of those did not return to use the buses after the strike.

In his Annual Report, the Chairman identified the private car as the most serious abstractor of traffic, expressing concern that, with the massive increase in cost that had faced the Company since the war, there was a danger of pricing themselves out of the market. He was also at pains to point out that the increased costs had not been wholly passed on to the travelling public. They had been partly absorbed by the Company, or mitigated by increased efficiency, constantly seeking ways of reducing cost, through introducing mechanical aids, and reducing waste mileage by regularly reviewing operations to eliminate journeys that were no longer well used. An example of this was the seasonal service 75 (formerly 140) running on Sundays between Hucknall and Gunthorpe on Sundays, which was not reinstated for 1957. Following from this, companion service 75A (formerly 141), from Bilborough, was renumbered 75.

The Company had been investigating the idea of spray painting vehicles, but it was decided at the time that this would not be economical, although it was adopted some years later, under different circumstances, to be described in due course.

However, the 1953 PD2s were, by this time, due for repaint, and three, 1238, 1239 and 1246 received an experimental livery of all over red, although a cream band was later added above the

lower deck windows. One single deck vehicle, Weymann bodied Tiger Cub 827 also received an all red livery, with a cream band below the windows, for which purpose suitable mouldings were added to the bodywork. However, all four vehicles reverted to standard livery at their next routine repaint.

More Metro-Cammell bodied PD2s were delivered in 1957, 34 in number, 1000-33, KCH 100-33, identical to the previous year's highbridge deliveries, and a further seven Burlingham Seagull bodied Tiger Cub coaches, although this time of centre entrance layout. The double deckers enabled more of the rebodied pre war Daimlers, and the last of the utilities to go, a total of thirty- nine vehicles leaving the fleet.

There was an interesting incident relating to the Daimlers. Reference was made in Chapter One to

the maintenance difficulties experienced after the war. However, this was also coloured by the experience of those involved. One foreman was ex army with desert experience. In the desert, parts had been difficult to obtain and due to this experience his approach tended towards making do with whatever was available.

Repairs were therefore made whenever possible, and this included repairs to the front wings of the pre-war Daimlers. Damaged pieces were cut out, new pieces welded in, made good and repainted. However, when the vehicles were eventually sold in 1956, brand new front wings were brought out of the stores, loaded onto lorries and taken to Frank Cowley at Salford, the well known dealer, who was buying the vehicles!

1238, one of the three 1952 PD2s that received an overall red livery at first repaint, on an experimental basis in 1957-8. Originally, they had been all red, after the style of neighbouring Midland Red, but the cream band was soon added. It will be recalled that an all red livery had been used briefly in the early post war years. The vehicles reverted to the standard livery at the next repaint. Later, the under canopy area was painted red and then the windscreen also, on half cab vehicles but, apart from this, there was no livery change until 1972.

Traffic congestion is not a modern phenomenon! By the early sixties, the Company was regularly complaining about the adverse effect of congestion on its operations. This 1962 view of Corporation Street in Derby, shows three of the Company's vehicles, a 1953 PD2, a 1958 PD3 and a 1951 Royal Tiger, caught in the evening peak hour traffic. Whilst the later construction of St Alkmund's Way, around the turn of the decade, removed much through traffic from the centre of Derby, traffic congestion is, at a time of writing, a worsening problem. Note, in the background, the 1957 Park Royal bodied Daimler CVG6 of Derby Corporation in Tenant Street, and the lengthy queue of potential passengers. This was the boarding point for Trent service 14 to Chaddesden Roosevelt Avenue, one of the services that the Company operated jointly with Derby Corporation.

Chapter Four
High Capacity Vehicles 1958-64

During 1958, twenty of the forty-three AEC Regals dating from 1946/7 were extensively modernised. These vehicles had 35 seat bodies with built in luggage boots and were used on seaside express services during the summer, but as they were just ordinary buses, this led to continual complaints from passengers. As many of the Regals had low mileage, it was decided that they should be modernised, and the first vehicle to be treated was 757, RC 9663, which had suffered accident damage.

The company also received twenty-two new vehicles during the year, these being 1034-55, LRC 434-55, the Leyland PD3/4 double deckers ordered in 1956. They carried Willowbrook H72RD bodies incorporating many of the lightweight principals featured in the Metro-Cammell Orion bodies delivered previously on PD2/12 chassis, but were rather better proportioned, not least because of identical depth windows on both decks, curved inward tapering sides and additional length. The seating capacity, at 72, was considerably higher than the 59 seats of the Metro-Cammell bodied PD2s delivered the previous year, and an even greater increase on the 56 seats of the Leyland bodies of 1955. They were the Company's first High Capacity Vehicles, and were so designated.

The chassis incorporated the same 0.600 engine as the PD2s, coupled to a constant mesh gearbox, and the vehicles had a particularly sporty exhaust note, which was quite distinctive, although a batch of PD2s delivered to Nottingham City Transport at the same time sounded similar, due to a new type of exhaust silencer. They had full air pressure brakes, compared with the vacuum brakes of the PD2s, and were the last front engine deckers delivered to the Company, but they

were excellent vehicles, and some were to have a long service life with Trent.

Although bulk withdrawals took place in 1971, after a fairly normal service life of 13 years, several were not finally withdrawn until 1977. 1054, in particular, led a charmed life, being withdrawn from service in 1972 and reinstated, withdrawn again in 1976 and then reinstated, finally being withdrawn from service in 1977. It was then used as a driver trainer for about ten years, before being preserved by the Company. When new, they displaced the last of the rebodied single deckers, SOS DONs and AEC Regals, the last rebodied pre war Daimler double deckers, whilst a start was made on withdrawal of the rebodied pre war AEC double deckers. Several of the SOSs were sent by

Cowley, the dealer, to Canada for forestry service.

An interesting event concerning these, however, was that two of the pre-war rebodied AEC Regents, 1163/4, RC 4631/2 which had been sold to the dealer, F Cowley of Salford, returned on hire or loan. During this returned period, the vehicles carried sign written painted fleetnumbers, in white numerals, as the original number plates had been destroyed at the time of the first sale. They returned to Cowley at the end of the year.

The withdrawal of forty-nine vehicles was matched by an intake of only twenty-two. It is significant that more vehicles were withdrawn than were delivered new, and this was partly indicative of the fall in traffic, which had started a year or two previously. There were many reasons

An interesting development in 1958 was the lengthening and conversion to full front and dual purpose specification of twenty of the 1947 AEC Regals. These had low mileage but looked old fashioned, and when used on seaside express services and excursions, their bus style interiors led to complaints. The conversions were quite effective from a passengers viewpoint, and the finished appearance not unattractive, with the moulding design clearly derived from the 1xx series Willowbrook bodied Tiger Cubs of 1953/4.

Various new methods were introduced in order to contain the continued increase in costs. Amongst these was the introduction of steam cleaning for chassis. 1335, RC 4633, one of the pre-war Regents with post-war Willowbrook body was photographed on the steam cleaning rig newly installed at Uttoxeter New Road depot in the late 1950s. The bus had only a few more months remaining service life with the Company, being withdrawn in 1959.

for this. Ordinary people were becoming better off, and were buying televisions. This meant that they no longer went out for entertainment, and cinema journeys by bus were no longer made. Changes in employment had caused more people to work a five day week, and they also had longer and more holidays. These factors led to both a decline in bus usage, and also a decline in the number of cinemas, with many town centre sites closing. The resurgence of the cinema at the time

of writing is a comparatively recent phenomenon, largely based around car borne patrons visiting multi screen cinemas at out of town sites.

Credit restrictions had been relaxed, and people were buying cars and motor scooters, so they were no longer interested in bus travel, preferring door to door convenience. There was also an upsurge in the availability of consumer goods, such as washing machines, competing for the public's cash. This left less to be spent on travel, although

the programme of extended coach cruises continued to be well patronised, and the end of Saturday working in many industries, particularly coal mining, also had an effect on revenue.

All of this put the Company's traffic under pressure, and this had been added to by successive fares increases, which had helped to drive passengers away, although it proved possible to avoid a fares increase in 1958. Economies were effected wherever possible, and as newer, more reliable vehicles were delivered, the periods between docks and overhauls could be extended. A steam-cleaning unit was installed at Derby for chassis cleaning, and new, more efficient bus washing machines were installed.

There were, however, some positive developments, for a new town service was introduced at Derby, 27, serving Breadsall (Scarborough Rise), a new housing development, and operating jointly with Derby Corporation on the basis carefully developed in 1948. A group of new services numbered 67A, 69, 69A and 70 were also introduced from Nottingham, to serve the new Grange housing estate at Gedling. In April, the new Borrowash Bypass was opened on the A52 between Nottingham and Derby, and this enabled the introduction of a new hourly non-stop service, X42 between the two centres. Trent's "good friends Barton Transport", to quote the Company Chairman, were joint operators on this service, which was only to be expected, and they used the same service number. Reference has already been made to the cordial relations which by now existed between the one time rival operators. The service proved highly successful, and today forms part of the Red Arrow and Trans Peak branded services.

Another new express service started was X24, Loughborough-Llandudno, via Nantwich, Prestatyn, Rhyl, Abergele and Colwyn Bay, and a further period excursion started was Wirksworth-Blackpool. Additions to the Blagreaves Lane services were some journeys serving Oaklands Avenue, using service numbers 49A and 51A.

In the springtime, Mr R C Hunt, who had been Chief Engineer since before the war, retired. He was succeeded by Mr P H Wyke Smith, who was later to achieve prominence in the industry as Chief Engineer of the National Bus Company.

The first new vehicles to arrive in 1959, were ten Leyland Tiger Cub PSUC1/2 models with Willowbrook DP41F bodywork. By the end of the year, the first Leyland Atlanteans, twenty-two in number, had been delivered and entered service, these being PDR1/1 models, eleven, 1056-66, ORC 656-66, with Metro Cammell H78F bodies, and eleven, 1358-68, ORC 758-68, with low height Weymann H73F bodies. Both low height and normal height bodies were based on the Orion design, described earlier. As a result of these arrivals, ten of the lowbridge rebodied 1937 AEC Regents and the first of the 1946 AEC Regals were withdrawn. The 1948 Windover bodied coaches were also disposed of, along with some of the ex-Naylor's vehicles.

A further fares increase was implemented from 21st June, 1959, the first for some twenty-one months, confined to increases on sub-standard and concession fares. However, the upward pressure on costs continued, with the Trade Unions lodging a national claim for a 40-hour working week and a 50% premium for one person operation (known in those days as one man operation!), this being completely rejected by the employers side, in the first instance.

The Company entered the forefront of the development of fluorescent lighting for buses and coaches in 1959, with fluorescent lighting conversions to 1958 PD3 1038, and newly delivered Tiger Cub 152, plus Metro Cammell bodied PD2 1002. This work, undertaken on behalf of the BET Group, led to the next deliveries of Atlanteans, and all subsequent vehicles, being fitted with this type of lighting, which gave much improved illumination levels and reduced usage of battery current, but the fitment of an alternator, in place of the dynamo, also brought about a major improvement. Additionally, 1038 had an illuminated advertisement panel on the off side, which enabled the value of advertising revenue to be increased. This development spread throughout the industry to most large operators, including that most conservative of undertakings, London Transport, which had many Routemasters fitted with such advertisement panels from new. However, in time, it was found that advertisers were unwilling to pay additional fees to justify the cost of illumination and the development fell by the wayside after several years, as one of those blind alleys which sometimes occur, most operators replacing the illuminated advertisement panel with plain panels. However, it had been an interesting development which reflected much credit on the company's staff, and generated a good deal of interest at the time, the vehicles concerned being driven to London's Victoria Coach Station for display to the industry. Whilst not the first application of fluorescent lighting for buses, this was the first application leading to full scale use and was, therefore, a pioneering development.

Central Works had also been engaged in another activity in converting former bus 751, one

1038, LRC 438 was the Company's pioneer vehicle in the development of fluorescent interior lighting and internally illuminated exterior advertising. The advertisement was made up of Perspex panels and the bodywork modifications needed to display it were carried out in Central Works. Such was the significance of the development that the vehicles were taken to London for display to bus and advertising industry representatives, and the vehicle was photographed at London's Victoria Coach Station, where the other prototype vehicles were also taken. Although the fluorescent tubes are visible inside the upper deck, so too are the original lighting units, which were subsequently plated over.

of the 1946 AEC Regals, into a lorry for carrying Company heavy plant and stores. It was a well designed vehicle, which received a grille of the type fitted to contemporary AEC goods vehicles to give a modern appearance. It replaced the previous lorry, 11, VO 5594, which had previously been bus 1202, acquired before the war with the business of Dutton's Unity Service of Nottingham.

There were few changes to services during the year, these being only minor. However, the business of G Howlett & Son (Quorn) Ltd, operating between Loughborough and Barrow on Soar and Sileby was offered, but Trent decided not to buy, as the price was too high.

Early in 1960, the Chief Engineer Mr P H Wyke Smith left the Company for a similar post at neighbouring North Western, which was a larger fleet, and was replaced by Mr V J Owen, who had worked for the Company previously as Assistant Chief Engineer.

A further 34 Leyland Atlanteans were delivered during the year, in various batches. These were, 1067-89, RRC 67-89, with Roe H78F bodies, 1369-73, SRC 369-73, with Weymann L73F bodies, similar to those delivered previously, and, later in the year, 1090-95, TCH 90-5, with further Roe H78F bodies. The chassis of 1067-89 were stored at Uttoxeter New Road for a while, due to problems at the body builders. Apart from a few utility bodies, Roe was a new supplier to Trent, but these vehicles did not have the traditional, and elegant timber framed body for which the builder was so well known. Rather, they had a steel framed body based on a design developed at the behest of BET by parent company Park Royal for the AEC Bridgemaster. 1095 was exhibited in the Commercial Motor Show at Earl's Court. They were equipped with fluorescent interior lighting, and 1069/71/80/1/3 also had illuminated an advertisement panel on the off side between decks panels.

Five new tour coaches, 229-33, RRC 229-33 had AEC Reliance chassis, rather than the Leyland Tiger Cub that had been favoured in recent years, with Weymann bodywork.

The total of forty-nine new vehicles enabled

the withdrawal of no less than seventy-nine older vehicles. These included the last of the 1937 AEC Regents with 1948 lowbridge bodies to go, along with more of the post-war Regals and the last ex Naylor's double decker was also withdrawn. Also a start was made on withdrawing the post war AEC Regents. One of the Regals, 746, was converted for use by the Cheshire Home at Staunton Harold, by the fitting of double doors at the back and removal of seats. It was repainted and named Crusader, starting a tradition, which was to extend through three vehicles, before the home eventual-

ly became a Sue Ryder Home. The chassis of this vehicle is now in the hands of a well known preservationist who specialises in high quality restoration of AECs.

During May, the company had a Dennis Loline with East Lancs body on demonstration. It was North Western 818, RDB 818, fitted with Leyland 0.600 engine and one of a batch of fifteen that had been placed in service earlier in the year. However, no orders for Dennis resulted.

A further fares increase, the ninth since the war, was implemented from 28th June 1960, but by

The new Leyland Atlanteans were quite revolutionary when first introduced and something rather different for the travelling public, as well as providing, at 78 seats, the highest passenger capacity to date for a main stream vehicle. The first supplied to Trent had Metro-Cammell and Weymann bodywork, but these were followed by two batches with the ungainly looking Roe bodywork illustrated here. For some reason, Roe painted the first few vehicles in Yorkshire Traction livery, as shown, but this was very soon corrected and normal Trent livery applied. 1066, RRC 66, awaits service on the joint Derby Corporation/Trent service 27 to Scarborough Rise, introduced some eighteen months or so previously. Note the legend "Town Service" on the blind, necessary because Trent vehicles were not normally allowed to both pick up and set down within the defined Corporation area.

The Company tried out one of North Western's Dennis Lolines for a spell during 1960. This particular vehicle had a Leyland 0.600 engine which would have been familiar at Trent, but the Loline was essentially the Bristol Lodekka built by Dennis under licence for the private sector, as Bristol and ECW could only supply to the state owned companies. Although long established, Dennis was, at that time, something of a niche builder of buses, being more successful with fire appliances and refuse freighters. No orders from Trent resulted, and indeed the number of orders from elsewhere was small. It was to be many years before Dennis became a main stream bus builder, as it is at the time of writing.

way of potential cost savings, national agreement was reached with the Trades Unions concerning one person operation. Drivers would be paid a 15% supplement for this type of work, and there was also a joint resolution by both the employers and the union sides to facilitate this form of operation. This was accompanied by the highest ever settlement on wage increases and shorter working hours. However, despite this agreement, the path to one-person operation was to prove a long one for Trent, and was not fully achieved until well into the seventies. Indeed, the issue of one-person operation was frequently raised with the Company's policy witness, when requests for increased fares came before the Traffic Commissioners.

In September, Mr S Ferry, who had joined the Company in August 1920 as assistant to the General Manager, retired from the post of Traffic Manager, to which he had been appointed in 1923. He had thus been with the Company through most of its formative years and, along with Mr G C Campbell-Taylor, General Manager from 1923 to 1946, made a major contribution to the Company. Mr D G F Rawlinson succeeded him, but the days of chief officials serving long periods were over, for the time being. Posts were now normally seen as a step on the career ladder, people staying long enough to gain the experience necessary for the next promotion, and then moving on when such a promotion opportunity presented itself. In some ways, this was a pity, but times had changed, and at least it ensured new blood bringing in ideas from elsewhere, and taking a fresh look at things.

On 1st February 1959, a payment was made to Midland Red in respect of 20% of the business of Boyer of Rothley, which they had recently acquired, operating between Leicester and Loughborough, via Rothley. On 8th April 1961 Midland Red handed over to Trent their X63 Leicester-Derby via Loughborough service. Trent combined this with service 625/6, but as this was joint with Midland Red, the change was, perhaps, only readily noticeable by the public on the Loughborough-Derby section

The Company carried 3/4 million fewer passengers during the year, as the trends previously outlined continued. However, this disguised the continuing good business on extended tours, on which bookings reached record levels, and also the fact that the mileage was still 50% higher than immediately before the war. The former North's service to Shottle had been extended to Cross o' th' Hands, but this proved unsuccessful, and it was cut back again to Shottle for the June 1960 timetable.

A new service, numbered 126 was started, running from Loughborough-Willoughby, via Midland Station, Cotes Corner, Hoton and Wymeswold.

Early in 1961, it was decided to place orders for 20 Reliance coaches, 20 Tiger Cub dual-purpose vehicles, or semi coaches in company parlance, and ten more low height Atlanteans. However, this was later changed to full height Atlanteans, and only four Reliances materialised for 1962. In the meantime, new deliveries for 1961 comprised fifteen PSUC1/1 Tiger Cubs, with Willowbrook B45F bodies, 830-44, VCH 830-44, fifteen PSUC1/2 Tiger Cubs with Willowbrook DP41F bodies, 162-76, VCH 162-76, and four AEC Reliances with Burlingham C41F coachwork. All the Tiger Cubs had bodywork of similar outline to the 1959 vehicles, but the dual-purpose vehicles featured luggage boots, a more elaborate livery, with swept side mouldings and greater areas of ivory. The Reliances marked a return once again to Burlingham, which had by this time been taken over by Duple, but the bodywork was to the Seagull 70 style, although this bore no resemblance to the classic Seagull design. Coach 45 was fitted with a ZF six- speed gearbox, the first in the fleet.

Twenty-seven vehicles left the fleet as a result of these new deliveries. All of the attractive 1950 AEC Regal llls left in one go - with the advent of the underfloor engine vehicles, they looked old fashioned and, with 33 seats, their capacity was rather low. Six of the 1951 Leyland bodied Royal Tigers also left, along with the solitary Burlingham bodied AEC Regal IV, acquired from Naylor's. The Royal Tigers seemed to have rather limited use latterly, and although painted into bus livery, their centre entrances meant that they were not really ideal for this purpose. Two of the 1955 Tiger Cubs, 131/47 received a reversed livery and revised moulding scheme, but this was not repeated on any of the others.

In March 1961, a further interhiring agreement came into operation, this time with Southdown, and the purpose of this was particularly, although not specifically, in connection with Trent's South Coast and Isle of White Tour, and was doubtless intend to enable a substitute vehicle to be readily available, in the event of breakdown.

During April 1961, Leyland Leopard L1 demonstrator, WJU 406, with Willowbrook DP41F body was loaned to the Company. The L1 Leopard was essentially a Tiger Cub chassis with the 0.600 engine in place of the latter's 0.375, but further Tiger Cubs, twenty in number, were ordered.

The downward spiral in the Company's fortunes, from its peak in the mid-fifties, continued. Wages were again increased, and a further fares increase was imposed from 2nd July 1961, but passengers were down by some 4%, as the number of cars on the roads increased, and Company profits fell. A bright area, however, was the Company's extended tours programme, which continued its success, in an area where it had established an excellent reputation.

Towards the end of the year, the South Normanton garage, acquired in 1956 with the business of E Naylor & Sons was sold as it was in a poor state of repair and little future use was seen for it.

Under the Transport Act 1962, there were changes in the arrangements for the state owned shareholding in the Company. The British Transport Commission was disbanded and its various transport functions assumed by new Boards. However, in the case of the English and Welsh bus holdings, these were taken over by a new, state owned Transport Holding Company (THC), which thus assumed ownership of the fifty per cent shareholding in Trent. Outwardly, there was little change but, unfortunately, there were no longer any railway Directors on the Board of the Company, and the Standing Joint Committee was disbanded.

In June 1962, the fleet was renumbered, with the object of containing each type of vehicle within a definite number range, so that the type of vehicle could be easily recognised from its number. This had been rather lost sight of in numbering vehicles over the years, although the fleet had been numbered in blocks since the system was introduced by the then new General Manager, G C Campbell- Taylor in 1923. The new scheme used was as shown below:

1-99	Coaches
100-99	Dual purpose vehicles 30ft long
200-99	Dual purpose vehicles 36ft long
300-49	Single deck buses 36ft long
350-99	Single deck buses 30ft long
400-599	Double deck buses high capacity
600-99	Double deck lowbridge buses
700-99	Double deck buses medium capacity

This scheme enabled the 41 seat dual-purpose vehicles to retain their existing numbers, whilst a few other vehicles, due for imminent disposal were also not renumbered.

At the same time, use of the colour plate numbering system, first introduced in 1923, was abandoned, the new plates being smaller, made of plastic, cream in colour and with the number printed in black. However, the Company found a continuing need to identify the allocation on the vehicles and coloured disc stickers were introduced, the following year, placed on the driver's windscreen. This evidently proved unsatisfactory, for use of the discs was discontinued after a few months. The colours varied somewhat from those used previously, being:

Alfreton	yellow
Ashbourne	silver
Belper	black
Meadow Road	brown
Uttoxeter New Road	pink
Hucknall	orange
Loughborough	blue
Mansfield	light green
Nottingham	dark green
Melbourne	gold
Shipley	white

The year's deliveries were the first new vehicles numbered into the new system. They consisted of four more AEC Reliance tour coaches, 43-6, YRC 43- 6, with Harrington

Twenty Alexander bodied Tiger Cubs arrived in 1962, as illustrated by this official portrait of three of them. Broadly similar to the Willowbrook bodied vehicles supplied the previous year, the deep panel for the destination box, and lack of opening windows made them instantly recognisable.

Cavalier C37F coach work, twenty Leyland Tiger Cubs with Alexander DP41F bodywork, 177-96, YRC 177-96, and ten more Leyland Atlanteans with Weymann H77F body- work, 462-71, 62-71 ACH. The Harrington Cavalier coachwork on the Reliances was another classic coach design, proving very popular in the industry, being specified by many BET companies, but also selling quite effectively into the independent sector.

The Tiger Cubs marked another new body supplier for Trent, but Alexander, which had previously supplied bodies almost exclusively in its Scottish homeland, was making serious sales inroads further south, logging major orders for the BET Group. The body was to the standard BET outline, as supplied previously to Trent by Willowbrook, and the livery was similar to the 1962 dual purpose Tiger Cubs supplied by that Company, although with detail differences.

As a result of these thirty-four new vehicles, some forty were withdrawn, a start being made on disposing of the 1948 Regent II double deckers, and the first of the 1958 rebuilt Regal dual purpose single deckers. The last of the Leyland bodied Royal Tiger coaches also left, and the entire 1952 batch of Leyland bodied Royal Tiger buses.

The new Atlanteans were the first Trent vehicles with reversed registrations, but also introduced a new three section destination box, with the usual three track route number blinds and final destination blind but with an additional and separate blind for intermediate destinations, of which two were usually shown.

A new Express service, started for the 1962 season, was the alteration of the period excursion from Alfreton and Derby to Rhyl to a service, X25, Alfreton-Llandudno, via Ripley, Belper, Derby, Mickleover, Rhyl, Abergele and Colwyn Bay, operating on hire to Crosville between Rhyl and Llandudno, using their licence. This was in furtherance of Crosville policy of always seeking a share in any new incoming traffic.

In March 1962, the combined businesses of Viking Motors and Victoria Motorways, of Burton on Trent were offered to Trent, and also to Midland Red. The two General Managers agreed that the two companies would share the business, but that Trent would negotiate. Little progress was made, and the combined businesses were offered again in 1967, but again, nothing came of the discussions.

Mr W Leese left the General Manager's post for the similar post at the larger, neighbouring North Western company, and was replaced by Mr J H Richardson, who joined the Company from smaller neighbour East Midland.

1963 was the Company's Golden Jubilee Year, and in September, a celebratory lunch took place at the Kings Hotel, Derby. A commemorative brochure was produced, describing aspects of the Company's history, and a special celebratory cover was used for the year's timetable books. Sadly, Mr J C Moth, who was a founder director of the Company, died on 28th January, just a few months before the anniversary. His connections with the Company went back to Commercial Car Hirers and he had been involved from the very start.

The United Counties Omnibus Company based in Northampton had, since acquiring the licence from Allchin & Sons of Northampton in 1933, been providing a daily express service between Nottingham, Leicester, Northampton and London. With an end to end journey time of around five hours the service, whilst acceptable as a cheaper alternative to rail travel, it had never carried any really significant weight of traffic until the advent of the M1 Motorway in 1959.

The first section of the M1, up to Crick near Rugby, enabled an hour to be taken off the through journey time and as further sections were opened up towards Nottingham in 1963, the development potential for the United Counties service became apparent. There was however, an operating problem in that the service was controlled from Northampton and with the steady increase in traffic originating in Nottingham and Leicester it became increasingly difficult to forecast the level of duplication that might be required. This sometimes totalled three or more duplicates in addition to the service vehicle.

The main concern was that confirmations of bookings made by agents along the Nottingham-Leicester section often did not reach the Northampton chartroom until after the time booked for the passenger to travel, and were therefore of no use at all when eventually received. United Counties made every effort to allocate duplication in line with estimated needs, but with a cautious approach this only too often meant overloads which involved delays to departures whilst emergency hiring arrangements were concluded. On the other hand, over-provision of duplicates could mean unnecessary dead mileage to and from Northampton and at 120 miles per round trip in the case of Nottingham this was an expensive exercise.

At that time United Counties garaged two or three of their vehicles overnight at Trent's depot in Nottingham and relations between the two Companies were quite cordial. This had recently superseded United Counties' earlier arrangements under which Robin Hood (Coaches) Ltd had garaged United Counties coaches at their Huntingdon Street premises, an arrangement that could have dated back to the days of Allchin & Sons, when Robin Hood were at West Bridgford.

The take-over of Robin Hood by Barton, which was effective from 31st December, 1962, although Barton had controlled the business from October 1961, did not include the Robin Hood premises, which the latter company had rented and not owned. Barton did not then have the space or facilities available to deal with United Counties vehicles, and hence United Counties turned to Trent for assistance. In addition to Nottingham, Trent, of course, also had a depot at Loughborough, and almost all the United Counties booking agencies in the sector also covered Trent's own express operations that were charted at Huntingdon Street.

In the circumstances, Trent were well placed to provide support in respect of the Nottingham-Leicester section of the London service by exercising some supervision over charting and also by the provision of duplicates to match traffic requirements. Agreement was reached that Trent/United Counties agencies would send confirmation of bookings made for the London service to the Trent chartroom in Nottingham either on

Trent buses or, in the case of late bookings, by telephone. Trent staff would then collate the information on a journey by journey basis and pass the bulk figures to the main United Counties chartroom in Northampton. This, when added to the detail already held there, would enable a far more accurate assessment to be made of duplication requirements which could then be passed back to Trent to implement.

An interesting development took place here in that the chartrooms of Trent at Huntingdon Street Nottingham and United Counties at Derngate Northampton were linked by Telex which allowed for an immediate transmission of the booking figures and duplication requirements between the two operators. This was a pioneering development, and London (Victoria), Cheltenham, Exeter, Bristol and Harrogate soon followed this initial link, it being generally agreed that the use of Telex in this field was of great benefit and achieved substantial economies in vehicle utilisation.

Inevitably, as both United Counties and Midland General were owned by the THC, whilst Trent was in the BET group, Midland General did not take at all kindly to the Trent/United Counties link-up and made very angry noises at the time! However, as they did not have any depots or agency facilities anywhere near the Nottingham-London route, nor at that time did they own many vehicles suited to Motorway operations, their objection could not reasonably be sustained and was therefore over-ruled. An interhiring agreement with United Counties came into operation from January 1964, doubtless to assist with the operation of this service.

Towards the end of the year 1963, the Company was examining double deckers available on the market, receiving a visit in October from Leyland Atlantean demonstrator SGD 669, a former Glasgow Corporation vehicle that had been repurchased by Leyland for use as a demonstrator. This was followed in November by 7552 MX, an AEC Renown demonstrator, and 171 NVO, a Leyland Albion Lowlander, which was D171 in the East Midland fleet. None of these visits resulted in orders for their manufacturer.

The overall box dimensions for buses had been

```
TRENTBUS NOTTM
UCOCO NPTON  -  AD 1: 63   11.0 A 14 MAR     TELEX LINK

TELEX LINK ESTABLISHED TODAY BETWEEN CHARTROOMS OF UNITED  COUNTIES
AND TRENT COMPANIES COULD WELL BE FIRST STAGE IN EXTENSIVE NETWORK
JOINING MAJOR EXPRESS OPERATORS.  TRENT CO-OPERATION APPRECIATED.
WELLMAN TRAFFIC MANAGER UNITED COUNTIES. +++  ?


TRENTBUS NOTTM  AD  1/63    14TH MARCH INTRODUCTION OF TELEX

TRENT HAPPY TO BE ASSOCIATED WITH UNITED COUNTIES

IN THIS IMPORTANT STEP TOWARD IMPROVING EXPRESS COACH
SERVICE TRAVEL.
RAWLINSON T.M.  TRENT


TRENTBUS NOTTM
UCOCO  NPTON +++
```

The inaugural telex that passed between Mr K H Wellman and Mr D G F Rawlinson, Traffic Managers of United Counties and Trent respectively, to mark the start of the pioneering telex operation for passing charting information between the two Companies in respect of United Counties' Nottingham-London service.

increased to 36′ long by 8′ 2½″ wide (10.98m by 2.5m) with effect from 1961, and the Company had soon placed an order for twenty four vehicles to the new dimensions. These materialised in 1963 as Leyland Leopards with Willowbrook DP51F bodywork of attractive appearance, 200-23, 200-23 CCH. They had a long service life, initially on front line express services, most lasting until 1978. 215 was loaned to Southdown for a period, for evaluation.

Ten double deckers delivered for 1963 marked a significant change of policy. It had been intended to order ten more Atlanteans, but the Daimler Fleetline had been giving a good account of itself elsewhere, and Birmingham City Transport Fleetline 3246, 246 DOC had demonstrated to the Company to good effect. This resulted in the decision to order Fleetlines instead, setting a pattern for the next ten years, or so.

The vehicles were 616-25, 616-25 CCH and the body order was also of interest, since these were H77F low height bodies by Northern Counties, another make which had never before featured in the fleet, but which was having some success outside its previous area of municipal orders. This was due to the fact that they produced a well proportioned body of good appearance, which also featured shrouds at the back to disguise the location of the engine compartment, although Trent subsequently removed these. Whilst generally noted for their sound construction, these bodies did give some trouble in Trent service. The body featured steel framing of top hat cross section with timber inserts into which the panel straps were screwed, and the screws were apt to work loose, with the passage of time, although the vehicles achieved a good service life. Following delivery of these vehicles, the fleet included, for a short period, vehicles registered CCH 620-5 and 620-5 CCH, until the former, 1951 Leyland PD2/3s, were withdrawn and sold.

Also delivered near the end of the year were three maximum length Leopard coaches, 1-3, 121-3 FCH with two speed rear axles and Plaxton C49F coachwork to their popular Panorama design. The new Fleetlines featured a dropped centre rear axle,

enabling a low height to be achieved and, as a result, these vehicles replaced the last ten low-bridge Willowbrook bodied AEC Regents, 1320-9. However, they provided a much better replacement as the rear axle allowed the elimination of the bench seats and the sunken gangway in the upper deck. Also withdrawn were the last of the 1958 rebuilt AEC Regals, the last Royal Tiger coaches, the last AEC Regent IIs and the last ex Naylor's vehicles, these being the two Reliance coaches that had set a new standard for Trent coaches.

Fares were once again increased during the year and although the rate of such increases had eased somewhat, this encouraged more people to buy cars, which in turn added to the Company's problems by increasing traffic congestion and hindering reliability of their services. Services were carefully and regularly reviewed to ensure best use was made of mileage run. For example, during the year, 18,000 fewer miles were run on the Ashbourne-Derby service, but an extra 50,000 miles were run on the Derby-Allestree services, where much new housing was under construction.

One consequence of new arrangements with United Counties for assistance with their London service, as described in the text, was the appearance of Trent vehicles at Victoria Coach Station in London on a regular basis. 211, 211 CCH, one of the newly delivered first batch of 36ft (10.97m) Leyland Leopards, with Willowbrook DP51F bodywork is shown parked at that location. Normally, a windscreen label reading "On Hire to United Counties" would be displayed, but this is absent, although visible in the two Trent Alexander bodied Tiger Cubs alongside. Note the recently adopted (and short-lived) new style destination display with, in this case, the "via" panel used for the message "Motorway Express".

The ten Daimler Fleetlines delivered in 1963 marked a new direction in vehicle policy for, in addition to the change from the previously delivered Leyland Atlantean chassis, they carried the first ever Northern Counties bodies, which were to a carefully detailed and well proportioned design, considered amongst the best supplied on rear engine chassis, at the time. The Fleetline chassis became the Company's standard, but no more Northern Counties bodies were ordered until some single deck vehicles on Volvo chassis were delivered in 1994. This newspaper photograph shows 625, 625 CCH, battling with flooding on the road between Burton and Hatton.

This was achieved with new services, 58, Derby-Allestree Lane (Robincroft Road), via Birchover Way, and 58A, Derby-Allestree (Woodlands Estate), via Birchover Way and Allestree Lane.

Around 1963/64, British Railways, under its Chairman Dr Richard Beeching, was reviewing its network with a view to identifying viable lines and dispensing with those that did not pay their way. Wholesale closures were proposed, and Dr Beeching achieved much notoriety as a result, to the extent that not all of the proposed closures were, in the event, allowed by the Government to be implemented. However, the impact of this on the bus industry was that in many cases, operators were called upon to provide replacement services.

There was much reluctance on the part of bus operators to do this for, almost inevitably, the services were doomed to failure, as they were designed to call at or near every station formerly served by the railway, with the result that they were slow and inconvenient. Unsurprisingly, particularly having regard to the fact that the railway services being replaced were little used any way, most were unsuccessful.

One service provided by Trent, and started on 7th September 1964 was a replacement for the service over the Great Northern line from Derby (Friargate) to Nottingham (Victoria), via West Hallam, Ilkeston, Awsworth, Kimberley and Basford, which was operated jointly with Midland General during Monday to Friday peak hours. Although the bus service served Huntingdon Street, which was the nearest bus station to the former Victoria Station (subsequently demolished to make way for the Victoria Shopping Centre), it actually terminated at Broad Marsh. However, the service was soon reduced to run between Nottingham and West Hallam, or Basford and Ilkeston, and was subsequently withdrawn altogether.

Express services continued to be developed, the following being new services for the 1964 season:

X27 **Nottingham-Cambridge,**
    via Melton Mowbray, Oakham, Empingham, Stamford, Peterborough and Huntingdon, on Fridays, Saturdays and Sundays.
    Jointly operated with Barton.
X28 **Derby, Nottingham-Felixstowe**
X29 **Derby, Nottingham-Southend,**
    via Melton Mowbray, Stamford, Biggleswade, Baldock, Hertford, Harlow, Ongar, Brentwood, and Southend Airport on Saturdays only.
    Jointly operated with Eastern National. Barton and Skills.
X31 **Barrow-Skegness,**
    via Sileby and Seagrave. Replacing the previous period excursion.

New deliveries for 1964 marked a return to Leyland for tour coaches, as there were five Leyland Leopard L2 (short models) with

In September 1964, British Railways (as it was then still known - the abbreviated title and well known double arrow logo were still a year or two into the future) finally withdrew the already very limited train service over the old Great Northern line between Derby Friargate and Nottingham Victoria, as part of the wide ranging service reductions proposed in the Beeching Report.

This handbill was distributed to provide information about the short-lived replacement bus service, designed to serve the station points on the line. The service was jointly operated by Trent and Midland General, and the omission of this information from the handbill is, perhaps, rather surprising.

British Railways Board
PUBLIC NOTICE
TRANSPORT ACT, 1962

Withdrawal of Railway Passenger Services

DERBY FRIARGATE and NOTTINGHAM VICTORIA

In accordance with the terms of the Minister's consent to the withdrawal of the above service, an additional bus service will operate commencing Monday, 7th September, 1964:—

TIME TABLE — Monday to Friday

	Read down	Read up	
	a.m.	p.m.	p.m.
DERBY (Friargate Station)	7.00	5.15	6.15
WEST HALLAM (White Hart) ...	7.19	4.56	5.56
ILKESTON (Bath Street/Station Road) ...	7.28	4.47	5.47
AWSWORTH (Keelings Corner) ...	7.35	4 40	5.40
KIMBERLEY (Y.M.C.A.)	7.39	4.36	5.36
BASFORD (David's Lane/Vernon Road) ...	7.46	4.29	5.29
NEW BASFORD (Meridian Works) ...	7.50	4.25	5.25
NOTTINGHAM (Broad Marsh)	8.00	4.15	5.15

These bus services to connect at Ilkeston Market Place with the existing bus service between there and Cotmanhay.

Passengers will be taken up and set down only at timetable stage points.

FARE TABLE — Return Fares only.

Derby						
—	West Hallam					
—	1/6	Ilkeston				
3/3	1/9	1/2	Awsworth			
3/6	2/3	1/6	—	Kimberley		
4/—	2/6	2/3	—	—	Basford	
4/—	3/—	2/5	2/2	1/10	—/9	New Basford
—	3/3	2/10	2/8	2/4	2/4	—	Nottingham

British Railways
LONDON MIDLAND REGION

BR 35000   August 1964   (AD 484)

significant supplier to the BET Group. The Alexander Y type was a very competent design making an attractive dual purpose vehicle, although the styling was, perhaps, too plain for a coach, despite its use as such elsewhere. Although there were no new double deckers delivered, twenty-six double deckers were withdrawn, these being the last AECs, the 1950 Regent Ills, and the first PD2s of 1951 and 1952. However, with 53 seats, the new saloons almost matched the 56 seat capacity of a double decker but, overall, there was a net reduction in the fleet size. The last Royal Tigers, with Willowbrook coach bodies, also left the fleet, and the first Burlingham Seagull bodied Tiger Cubs, as well.

A further demonstrator tried was 36ft (10.97m) long Bedford VAL14/ Willowbrook B53F 525 LMJ, with its unusual "Chinese six" twin-steer layout. This visited in March 1964 but, once again, no order was placed. However, a repeat order for five Leyland Leopard L1 coaches was cancelled, and replaced with an order not for VALs, but for six 30' (9.14m) Bedford SBs.

Late in the year, the Traffic Manager, Mr D G F Rawlinson left and was replaced by Mr J C Clymo, who later became prominent at BET Headquarters, as did Mr Rawlinson in the National Bus Company.

In December 1964, the business of W Gash & Sons Ltd, of Newark, was offered to the Company. In operational terms, Trent were very interested as the acquisition would have protected the vulnerable eastern flank of their area, provided a depot closer to the east coast and achieved considerable mileage savings. It was envisaged that the business would have been retained as a separate entity, but that the vehicles would have received Trent livery, as Gash's two tone green and cream was, surprisingly, not viewed as a strong point. There were some worries that the business might have been of interest to Mansfield District or Lincolnshire, but it was decided that the purchase was not worthwhile in terms of investment, and was not proceeded with. However, Lincolnshire eventually acquired Gash in 1989.

Harrington Grenadier C40F bodies. The Grenadier was a development of the Cavalier featuring a revised front panel and deeper windscreen, together with longer side windows. Also, eight maximum length Leopards with Alexander Y type C49F bodies, which vehicles were classified as dual purpose with fleet numbers 224-31, ACH 224-31B), and sixteen maximum length Leopards with Marshall B53F bodies, 300-15, ACH 300- 15B. Marshall was a long established company that had recently acquired the Birmingham firm of Mulliner, which had previously produced bodywork in small numbers for specialist markets. It developed this business, at its Cambridge base, to become a quite

Trent's early experience with high capacity double deckers, after the Leyland PD3s, had been with the then revolutionary Leyland Atlantean, Leyland having been the favoured main supplier since 1951. However, this proved to be fairly short lived and the Daimler Fleetline was the standard double decker for the greater part of the sixties at the end of the BET era and, indeed, for a few years thereafter. Most had the Alexander body work, as illustrated by 488, HRC 488D, one of ten delivered in 1966, and shown setting down down passengers in a partly completed Maid Marian Way in Nottingham. Close behind is a Barton Bedford VAL, with uncommon Harrington Legionnaire coachwork, operating on stage carriage work, despite the coach body - in the usual Barton style of the time.

Chapter Five
1965-68
The Final BET Years

In 1965, Mr J H Richardson left the General Manager's post, for another BET post and was succeeded by Mr L Waller. During that year, the coloured discs placed on vehicle windscreens to indicate depot allocations were replaced by discs placed adjacent to the front fleet number. The colours were, once again slightly different from those previously used, as listed below:

Alfreton	yellow
Ashbourne	silver
Belper	blue
Meadow Road	brown
Uttoxeter Road	red
Hucknall	black
Loughborough	orange
Mansfield	green
Nottingham	gold
Melbourne	red or brown
Shipley	red or brown

Melbourne and Shipley depots were, by now, considered to be sub depots of the two Derby depots, and carried discs coloured accordingly, rather than being allocated their own specific colour codes.

The company once again tried a demonstrator, this being Central SMT BL 273, EGM 273C, a Bristol Lodekka FLF6GLX with ECW H78F body. Bristol and ECW were again by now able to supply on the open market, following acquisition of a 25% a share in Bristol by British Leyland, but no order for Lodekkas was placed by Trent or, indeed, any other BET Company. However, new vehicles delivered for 1965 were ten Daimler Fleetlines with Alexander H78F bodies, 472-81, ECH 472-81C, and twenty more Leopards with Willowbrook bodies, 232-41, ECH 232-41C,

being DP49F, and 242-51, ECH 241-52C being DP5IF. The first ten had a moulding scheme similar to Alexander bodied 224-31, delivered in 1964, whilst the second ten had a moulding scheme and livery like 200-23, delivered in 1963. They were originally to have been bodied by Weymann, but the order was diverted to Willowbrook, at some extra cost, due to a prolonged strike at Weymann, which ultimately resulted in the factory being closed.

Also new were ten coaches, being four Leopards with Plaxton C49F bodies, 4-7, ECH 4-7C and six Bedford SB5s with Duple Bella Vega C41F bodies, 70-5, ECH 70-5C, for day excursion work. The Leopards were much as before, although the chassis were the first in the fleet to feature air suspension, and the bodies were of the updated Panorama style. The Bedfords, however, were something quite new to the Company, being

lightweight chassis, very similar to contemporary vehicles being supplied to independent operators, and the first of the make ever operated.

Finally new for 1965 were eight Leyland Tiger Cubs with Alexander Y type C41F bodies, 100-7, HRC 100-7C. It had been intended to order ten with B45F Alexander bodies, but the order was changed at an early stage. As with the maximum length Y types, the vehicles were numbered in the dual purpose, rather than coach series. This varied selection of vehicles led to the withdrawal of eleven PD2s of 1953, all of the 1955 Tiger Cub buses, and some more Tiger Cub coaches.

From 15th April 1965, the Company started a new express service between Alfreton and London via Derby, Loughborough and the M1 motorway, under the name" Derbyshire Express". This was jointly operated with Midland General, United Counties and Yelloway of Rochdale, using the

Perhaps the most surprising deliveries in 1965 were six Bedford SB5s with Duple Bella Vista bodies delivered for day excursions. This official view, taken when new, shows that the adaptation of the Trent livery suited the bodywork quite well. The vehicles were never popular with drivers, not least because many had difficulty in reaching the pedals. The engine also proved somewhat troublesome in Trent service. However, these factors did not prevent further Bedfords from being purchased, although these were of later models.

Ten of the twenty Willowbrook dual purpose Leopards delivered in 1965 featured an external moulding layout similar to that of the Alexander Y type bodywork delivered in the previous year. However, they also had two fewer seats, at 49, and were equipped with forced air ventilation, making them suitable for long distance travel. 238, ECH 238C was photographed in Nottingham some years after delivery, by which time a red skirt had replaced the previous ivory.

service number MX4 and giving Trent its first ever daily link by road with the Capital, from the railway stronghold of Derby, although Yelloway had, of course, operated since the thirties. The new service had been the subject of a long battle in the Traffic Court, mainly due to railway opposition, British Railways claiming an adequate service between London and Derby. This was despite the fact that it was intending to reduce this from 1966, following the electrification of the West Coast Main Line, which would provide a faster route from London to Manchester. Indeed, the line from Derby to Manchester was to be largely closed between Matlock and Buxton, except for a limited length at the Buxton end to serve quarry traffic.

The proposal had, however, started in 1964, with a joint application by Trent and United Counties for an Alfreton-London service.

Yelloway already had its long established daily service between Derby and London, which operated from Easter to the end of October, and also at Christmas, as part of its Blackpool/Blackburn-London routes. These services were not designed to cater for Derby-area people, but rather the timings were arranged to meet the needs of the vast number of passengers from Blackpool, Blackburn and Manchester. Despite this, Yelloway had carried 4,582 southbound passengers from Derby in 1963, of which over 500 used a night journey leaving at the inconvenient time of 2.43 am. Yelloway countered the Trent/United Counties application with an application of their own for an enhanced Derby-London service.

United Counties had its similarly long established and well known service between Nottingham and London via Loughborough,

Leicester and Northampton. This had no duplication limits on the licence, the bulk of the Nottingham-London direct traffic by then being carried on "flyers" using the M1 motorway between North London and Crick, as previously described. As also previously described, Trent had begun to participate in this service from 1963, by providing duplicate vehicles and charting assistance. These services were expected to become even speedier when the M1 was extended further north to Leicester and beyond. United Counties carried some 3,468 Derby area passengers to London, who travelled via Nottingham to use their service, whilst Trent and Midland General operated their stage carriage services which provided linking facilities from Alfreton to Derby and to Nottingham respectively.

There were, therefore, a range of interests, and the four operators agreed to jointly propose a daily return service from Alfreton to London, with another daily return journey London to Derby. Additionally it was intended to run extra journeys between Derby and Northampton on popular days, connections being made at Northampton to existing United Counties journeys to London. One of the points made on behalf of the four road operators was that the trains from Derby to London took up to 2 hours 20 minutes, hours compared with coach timing of 4 hours 15minutes. The appeal of the proposed service, therefore, would be to people already using coach facilities or those who would prefer to use road travel rather than go by train, which they had to do in the absence of any really convenient express coach service.

In the context of this application, it should be noted that, prior to the 1980 Transport Act, it was necessary for any operator applying for a new licence to demonstrate that there was a public need for the proposed service. British Railways and its predecessors were frequent objectors, particularly to proposals for long distance express coach services. Despite the number of passengers carried, as already described, the joint operators had difficulty in demonstrating the additional need, and the Traffic Commissioners held that what they had demonstrated was a need for improved connecting services between Alfreton and intermediate points to Derby or Nottingham. The Commissioners suggested the need could be met by a limited-stop service running once or twice a day from the Alfreton area "certainly into Nottingham and possibly into Derby." They further suggested that at Nottingham these journeys might connect with the most popular timings of the United Counties service and the busiest trains, calls being made at the largest of the Nottingham bus stations and at the busiest of the railway stations. This, however, ignored the fact that the terminals used by the bus and train operators were scattered over the City. United Counties terminated at Huntingdon Street, Midland General's Alfreton services terminated at Mount Street, whilst the principal London train service served Nottingham Midland which was in a third location. Although reference was made to the uncertainty of the rail services, the Traffic Commissioners were only prepared to consider the rail facilities as they existed at the time of the hearing. There was also the potential disadvantage that rail passengers from the Alfreton area would have had to re-book at Nottingham as the special monthly fare, and day-return or half-day tickets, were only available from there. Eventually, a licence was granted, but was limited by the Traffic Commissioners to one vehicle per day, the joint operators each running the service for three months in turn. The case serves to illustrate just how difficult it then was to obtain a licence to run a new bus or coach service, even when there was an obvious demand, prior to de-regulation and the elimination of road service licencing. Trent had one vehicle, a Leopard with Plaxton Panorama coachwork, allocated to Alfreton depot, and the service was considered by staff to be very much a prestige duty. When Yelloway took their turn at operation, their vehicle was out stationed at Midland General's Alfreton depot.

A new service, X34 from Derby to serve East Midlands Airport was started as a limited stop variation of the existing 34 service, but did not last very long, being withdrawn by 1967. An earlier version of this service had run from Nottingham,

The first Derbyshire Express timetable leaflet. There was one return journey per day, leaving Alfreton at 07.40 and returning at 20.10. Other journeys shown were some seasonal operations by Yelloway, and an evening journey leaving Derby for Northampton at 17.55, which connected with a seasonal service between Northampton and London. There was also an early morning service leaving Northampton at 07.30, arriving in Derby at 0951. The service was slow, because it travelled on all purpose roads, rather than the M1, between Derby and Northampton, serving Loughborough and Leicester.

Huntingdon Street, to the former Derby Airport at Burnaston. A few new stage carriage services were started in 1965, as shown below:

103, **Ripley-Ilkeston,**
via Denby, Kilburn, Horsley Woodhouse, Smalley and West Hallam Cross Roads on Saturdays, only.

107, **Ambergate-Ripley,**
via Nether Heage and Heage.

108, **Belper-Ripley,**
via Nether Heage and Heage.

134, **Shelthorpe-Bishop Meadow (Belton Road West Industrial Estate),**
a Loughborough Town Service.

The mobile booking office, no 23, RC 2721, formerly bus 321 and used at Skegness during the Summer months, was replaced by a caravan drawn by a Land Rover. It was sold for a nominal sum to the Lincolnshire Vintage Vehicle Society for preservation, where it remains at the time of writing, repainted in a version of Trent livery, but without the original seats due to its previous use, and used as a tea-room.

Staff wages were increased, and this was followed by a further general fares increase from 18th July 1965, these having remained unchanged for some two years, and traffic continued to fall. The peak year had been 1955 with 62.11 million passengers carried and 16.46 million miles operated, but by 1966, this had fallen to 45.41 million passengers carried, and 15.54 million miles operated. However, the number of passengers carried was still comparable with immediate pre-war levels, whilst the mileage operated was considerably higher than at that time.

By 1966, an agreement had been reached locally with the Trade Unions to introduce one person operation, this having been first subject to national agreement in 1958, but had met with local opposition. As a result of this, the Company's first one person operation service commenced in late June 1966, but subject to a maximum vehicle capacity of 45 seats.

During 1966, the business of Housden's of Loughborough was offered, and their position as premier operator of excursions from Loughborough was of some interest, especially viewed against the possibility of Barton buying it instead, but it was decided not to pursue the matter.

For the 1966 season, there were still more new express services:

X12 **West Hallam-Scarborough,**
via Bridlington and Filey.
Jointly operated with Midland General.

X23 **Manchester-Skegness,**
via Nottingham and Mablethorpe.
Jointly operated with North Western

X25 **Nottingham, Derby-Pwllheli.**
Jointly operated with Barton

X26 **Nottingham, Derby-Harlech,**
via Dolgellau and Barmouth.
Jointly operated with Barton

X27 **Loughborough, Derby-Llandudno**

X28 **Alfreton, Derby-Bangor,**
via Llandudno

During 1966, a start was made on relocating the fleetname on double deckers to the temple position immediately above the cab, or the comparable position on the nearside. At the same time, the front registration number plate on rear engine vehicles was relocated above the front windscreen. These changes were designed to minimise repair costs, in cases of accident damage.

New vehicles followed the by now familiar pattern, with eleven more Alexander bodied Fleetlines, 482-92, HRC 482-92D, and ten more dual purpose Leopards with DP51F bodywork, this time by Metro Cammell. There were also three Leopard coaches, on L2 chassis, with Plaxton Panorama C40F coachwork. These led to the withdrawal of many of the 1955 Tiger Cubs, as well as the first two 1957 Burlingham bodied Tiger Cub coaches, and two of the 1960 Weymann bodied AEC Reliance coaches.

In October 1966, the main part of the new development at Meadow Road, Derby, became

One of the 1963 Leopard/Panorama coaches travels along Corporation Street, Derby, on the new Derbyshire Express service. Note the headboard and the single blind carrying both destination and service number.

operational, being fully completed by the end of the year.

For the first time, in 1967, the Company was able to offer a large number of Continental holidays, covering a wide range of continental destinations in addition to its usual programme of UK destinations. This was in conjunction with sister BET Company Sheffield United Tours, which Company had a great deal of experience in this type of work, using their red and grey vehicles with trademark bright metal strips. Most of the holidays operated from East Midlands Airport, with pick-ups by Trent in most of the major towns in their operating area. In spite of this development, Trent's home programme, which had built up an excellent reputation over the years, was expanded with new destinations.

A new stage carriage service started in 1967 was 99A, Horsley-Ripley, via Cumbersome Corner, Denby and Marehay, and there were further express developments:

X30 **Nottingham, Derby-Barry Island**
X31 **Barrow on Soar-Skegness,**
     replacing the previous period excursion.
X33 **Manchester-Skegness** (Direct)
X92 **Nottingham, Derby-Liverpool,**
     via Ashbourne, Leek, Macclesfield, Knutsford, Warrington and Prescot, Jointly operated with North Western and Lancashire United.

The following year, in May, 1968, an interhiring agreement was entered into with Lancashire United, doubtless prompted by the start of the X92 service.

In April, 1967, the new, four storey office block in Uttoxeter New Road was occupied from 17th April, providing much improved accommodation for staff, previously used to working in a variety of old houses.

During the year, a start was made in introducing a new uniform for the road staff. It had been felt that the previous uniform was too military in appearance, which was no longer appropriate, and a new one was introduced with less detail and cut in a finer cloth which were considered to give a more civilian look and greater comfort to wear. A new plastic company badge was introduced in yellow on red, to replace the former metal one.

A Labour Government had been elected by a slender majority in 1964, and was re-elected in 1966 with a greatly increased majority. Mrs Barbara Castle was Minister of Transport in that government and had put forward a White Paper entitled "Transport Policy", containing proposals for public ownership of the industry, which the BET Group, initially, fought hard against. This brought some conflict of interest, for the Company was half owned by the Transport Holding Company, which was state owned and concerned about the possibility of being associated with anti

Roe bodied Atlantean 446, (originally 1080), RRC 80, illustrates the new "temple" position adopted for the fleetname on double deckers, and also the relocation of the front registration number plate above the windscreen. The vehicle is pictured at the junction of Albert Street with St Peter's Street and Cornmarket in Derby. The typeface used on the destination blind is non standard for Trent and, indeed is different from that used for the next destination, just visible at the top of the aperture.

Government propaganda. It did not wish to see the costs of such propaganda being a charge against its revenue interests, and requested that steps be taken to prevent this.

New vehicle deliveries were twenty of the by now standard Alexander bodied Fleetlines, 493-512, MRC 493-512E and a range of different coaches. 63-7, MRC 563- 7E were short Leyland Leopards with Plaxton C40F bodies, and 76-81, MRC 576-81E were Bedford VAM5 with Plaxton C41F bodies. Later in the year, these were joined by 8-11, PRC 208-11F, maximum length Leopards with Plaxton C49F coachwork to a new style. The last of the Leyland bodied PD2s were withdrawn, and also some of the Metro Cammell ones, as well

as more of the 1955 Tiger Cub dual purpose vehicles and the remaining Weymann bodied Reliance coaches.

The business of Stevensons of Uttoxeter was offered following the death of J Stevenson, but the Company declined to make an offer. Also during the year, in October, it was once again necessary to raise fares, for the fifteenth occasion.

The controversy over the government's proposals for extending state ownership of the bus industry had continued and been vigorously opposed by BET. However, faced with the seeming likely possibility of compulsory acquisition of at least part of its operations, especially the most profitable ones in the major conurbations, BET performed an about turn, and it was announced in October 1967 that its UK bus interests would be sold to the government. Whilst this was, to some extent, a surprise to observers at the time and, indeed, there were allegations of bad faith in some quarters, it must be seen against the perception that the economics of bus operation were becoming increasingly difficult, mainly for the reasons which have been outlined in earlier chapters. The licencing system at the time, based on the provisions of the 1930 Road Traffic Act, meant that operators had far less flexibility in adjusting their services than exist in the current climate. Also significant was a threat by Mrs Barbara Castle, Minister of Transport, to bring forward an Act of Parliament authorising compulsory purchase, which, if carried out, may have resulted in a lower payment for the BET bus undertakings. Taking all of the factors into account, the policy change perhaps looks less surprising when viewed from a distance of some thirty five years.

The effect of the sale was that on the 1st January 1968, control of Trent passed to the state owned Transport Holding Company. From the 1st March, 1968, Trent became a subsidiary of that Company, alongside the other former BET subsidiaries and joining the existing subsidiary Tilling Group Companies, including close neighbours Midland General, Notts & Derby and Mansfield District. This event placed Trent and these three companies in the same camp for the first time, which was to have far reaching effects, to be described later. However, there was initially no immediate and obvious effect from this change of ownership, and things appeared much as they had previously.

Relations between Trent and Midland General over the years had been very much influenced by the personalities of those involved in the respective managements. Unlike the later periods in BET, Tilling and NBC days, when managers tended to move on after two or three years in office, the senior management at both Trent and Midland General held the same positions through decades. This had applied particularly in the cases of the

Traffic Managers (Messrs Ferry of Trent and Laing of Midland General). It had been mainly at this level that a degree of friction between the two Companies had seemed to persist, and during their period of office co-operation was at a minimum. Appearances, one against the other, in Traffic Court were by no means infrequent.

There had been, however, an overall agreement reached by the General Managers - G C Campbell-Taylor of Trent and Douglas Hays of Midland General - which was supported by a map showing agreed frontiers and territorial spheres of operation. This agreement had always been honoured in principle by both parties and undoubtedly reduced any hostile exchanges to the level of "skirmishes" rather than any outright "wars".

In the post-war years, however, there had been some notable examples of co-operation between the two Companies on express services. When new destinations, other than the time honoured Blackpool and Skegness, were being sought, Trent and Midland General had worked together to Great Yarmouth, Scarborough and Clacton-on-Sea from Alfreton, Ilkeston and Mansfield.

With Stage Carriage operations there was little operational co-operation and there were still a number of cases where licence conditions imposed protective conditions on one or other of the two parties against the other, or where joint operation might have been possible but was not pursued. There had been a Traffic Court case of some substance involving the two companies as a result of Midland General seeking a new service via Watnall between Nottingham and the Beauvale Estate in Hucknall, which had found in favour of Midland General. However, in the case of fares, agreement was invariably reached over those which applied to common sections - for example, Mansfield - Sutton - East Kirkby when general increases were found to be necessary.

One memorable occasion when both Companies had co-operated very effectively was in the early post-war years when an Air Display attended by over 100,000 people was held at RAF Hucknall on a Bank Holiday Monday. Almost all attending this event had no alternative but to

The map opposite is a facsimile at reduced size of that which was included in timetable books in post war years. A similar format was used by other BET Group companies and shows British Railways lines and contact stations, as well as the Company's own services. It shows an approximation of the Company's route network towards the end of the BET era, although it may not be wholly accurate and one suspects that it was not updated significantly after the original block was made. The map makes an interesting comparison with the original area agreement map shown on page 39 of Part One. Little had changed, in terms of operating area since that time and there remains the large gap in the network around the Nottinghamshire/Derbyshire border occupied by Midland General and Notts and Derbys Traction. The area to the southwest of Nottingham, and other parts, remained largely the preserve of independent Barton. It was to be still another twenty or so years before Trent took full occupation of both of these areas.

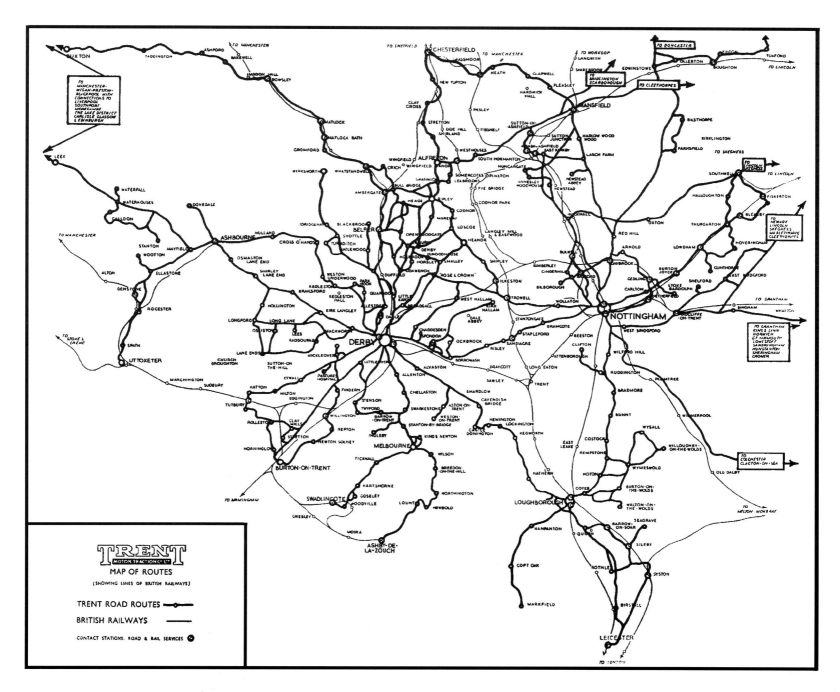

TRENT
MOTOR TRACTION Co. Ltd.

MAP OF ROUTES

(SHOWING LINES OF BRITISH RAILWAYS)

TRENT ROAD ROUTES ●—————●

BRITISH RAILWAYS ——————

CONTACT STATIONS. ROAD & RAIL SERVICES ⓒ

47

travel by public transport and a joint service was provided from Nottingham (Huntingdon Street) to Hucknall via Bulwell returning via Watnall and Cinderhill to Mount Street.

After the Air Display finished there was a queue of red and blue buses as far as the eye could see in both directions outside the RAF Station and, as a people moving exercise, it had been highly successful. Only one fare (1/- (5p) adult & 6d (2½p) Child) was charged and every available vehicle from both Companies was pressed into service. Legend has it that it took the rest of the week to count the cash receipts from this operation!

As previously mentioned, the era of senior officials remaining in post for years had long finished. With the passage of time, and the fading of old rivalries, the levels of co-operation between the two neighbours improved considerably during the period leading up to the sale of the BET companies to the government, and this soon developed further.

Over the course of the next eighteen years, Trent was to operate as part of a state owned concern, subject to government policies of the day. A new standardised livery was adopted and the vehicles became highly standardised. Major expansion of the Company occurred with the take- over of the neighbouring Midland General fleet and part of neighbouring North Western. In the case of absorption of Midland General, this was in furtherance of National Bus Company policy, whilst the North Western takeover was in furtherance of government policy in relation to the provision of public transport in Greater Manchester. This expansion was, however, counterbalanced by the continual decline of passenger numbers. In 1986, the company was to return again to private ownership, but it is significant that, despite the large increase in operating territory, the number of vehicles owned in 1986 was little different from the number owned at the end of the BET era. The stories of the company's development under National Bus Company ownership, and its later return to private ownership will be told in subsequent volumes.

During the mid-sixties, the Company was very active in improving its properties in Derby, with major extensions at Meadow Road depot and the conversion of Uttoxeter New Road depot to a new Central works. Alongside the latter, a new four-storey office block was built, providing modern, purpose-built accommodation for Head Office staff. This picture was taken in April 1967, on completion of the building. It is still stands in Uttoxeter New Road, although no longer occupied by Trent, following relocation to the former Midland General Head Office building at Mansfield Road, Heanor, in 1996, a building of similar age.

The Vehicles

The fleet policy of standardisation, which was becoming more evident during the period 1935-40, resumed after the war. However, due to the fact that body styles and manufacturers changed every few years, this did not always appear to be the case. Certainly, in the fifties there was wide variety, which continued to some extent into the sixties, but by the end of that decade the appearance of new vehicles was becoming pretty consistent. This was particularly so in relation to single deck bodywork for which, from 1959, the standard BET designs were used, albeit supplied by different manufacturers and subject to development over a period of years, causing some variety of appearance. Different livery styles, featuring a greater area of ivory, were used on vehicles intended for dual purpose use, which also added variety.

Immediately after the war, the Company embarked on its major rebodying and new vehicle programmes, almost all of which featured Willowbrook bodywork to designs which developed over a period of about five years. AEC chassis were specified exclusively for new vehicles until 1950, but from 1951, there was a complete change, only Leyland chassis being specified until 1959, when other marques once again appeared. All of the home market Leyland chassis models during the fifties and early sixties featured in the fleet, and Leyland bodywork was specified, too, until body production at the the original Farington plant ceased. Thereafter, Metro-Cammell bodywork found favour for double deckers, followed by a brief return to Willowbrook, although the latter continued as a regular supplier of single deck bodywork throughout the period covered by this volume. In the early sixties, Roe briefly became a supplier, on Leyland Atlantean chassis, and by now double deck body design had sunk to an all time low, throughout the industry, save for the Tilling group which bought only well designed, if conservatively styled, ECW products. In the author's view, the Roe bodies had the worst appearance of any ever supplied to the Company, being badly proportioned and poorly detailed, but clearly built to achieve low weight.

The Scottish Alexander concern became a major force in bodybuilding during the nineteen sixties, a position which it retains, as part of Transbus, at the time of writing, having been helped over some of the leaner years by extensive orders from the erstwhile Scottish Bus Group and from the Far East. Most of the single deck dual purpose vehicles supplied by Alexander were to BET standard design, although featuring an external livery layout and moulding design that was unique to Trent, and including also a few of the suppliers own Y type design. The double deck Alexander bodies, of which many were supplied from 1965 onwards, were to a new design, first supplied to Glasgow Corporation, which featured curved glass windscreens on both decks, and made use of glass fibre reinforced plastic mouldings for some panels, both of which enhanced the appearance considerably. The Construction and Use Regulations had earlier been amended to eliminate the requirement for an opening windscreen and this, coupled with improvements in glass technology, first applied to private cars, allowed the use of curved glass and gave greater scope for styling. This feature first became evident on coaches, and the Burlingham Seagull 70 and classic Harrington Cavalier both introduced full width curved glass windscreens to the fleet. The Plaxton Panorama coach design also entered the fleet and this featured not only curved glass windscreens, but also introduced long side glass as well. On later versions, this, too, was curved, in the vertical plain.

The Daimler Fleetline took over from the Leyland Atlantean as the Company's standard double decker, introducing that marque to the fleet once again, and also the Gardner engine, after a gap of some six years. AECs also made a brief return to favour, for tour coaches, although when these arrived, many of the post war AECs still remained in the fleet. Despite the moves towards standardisation, some variety still remained in the fleet at the end of the period covered by this volume The selection of photographs that follows attempts to portray the vehicles featuring in the fleet over the period 1946-68.

Ten of the pre-war Daimler COG5s, originally fitted with Weymann bodies, were overhauled and rebodied during 1946, the new Willowbrook H54R bodies having rear entrances, rather than forward entrances, as had the originals. In general proportion and style, they owed much to the utility bodies supplied during 1942-3, when coach and single deck bus chassis had been rebodied. Although the rear dome was rounded, and some of the windows were heavily radiussed, the cab area, canopy and entrance, together with the completely parallel sides from front to back of the vehicle bore a close resemblance to those earlier bodies, suggesting that Willowbrook had not had time to undertake more than a minimal amount of design work before fulfilling the order. 1051, RC 6000, was originally new in 1938, and remained in the fleet until 1957. It is seen here in August, 1952, passing Sherwood's Metropole cinema, which nowadays is a Kwik Save supermarket. Note the multi barred telegraph pole, very much a characteristic of the era, and the pre-war Austin Seven saloon car.

Refurbished and Rebodied

During six long years of war, no new vehicles were delivered in 1941 and 1942, and only thirty-two in the years 1943-45. As a result, the fleet was tired, and many elderly vehicles had been retained beyond their normal working life. In addition to the many new vehicles that arrived in the post war years, A large number of the vehicles delivered between 1934 and the war were overhauled and rebodied. Vehicles of AEC, Daimler and SOS manufacture all received this treatment, the chassis overhauls being carried out in Central Works.

The first vehicles in the rebodying programme were the 1934 SOS ONs, which, early in 1946, lost their superb Duple Rodney express coach bodies. The chassis were thoroughly overhauled and the SOS petrol engines were replaced by new AEC 7.7 litre diesel engines,   making them effectively DON chassis. However, little else was done to upgrade the mechanical specification and, for example, the original rod brakes were retained. The aluminium plate at the lower edge of the radiator extended below the original bottom tank of the radiator, just beneath the starting handle boss. By post war standards, the depth was shallow and the radiator high mounted, but the plate helped to disguise this. The single aperture destination box was a continuance of pre war practice, and the route number, a three track blind unit in a wooden, varnished box, rather than stencils, as pre-war, was mounted on the front bulkhead, beneath the canopy. Note the duplicate sign beneath the canopy, which was a fold down, spring loaded unit. These were fitted from about 1948, to avoid the need to set the blind to read "Duplicate", which was removed from the blinds, along with the similarly unhelpful word "Service" and also "Not on Service".

Lowbridge AECs

No vehicles were rebodied in 1947, but in 1948, the programme restarted, and the 1937 AEC Regents shown in these photographs were rebodied with Willowbrook L55R bodies in 1948 and 1949 and renumbered. During the war, the Company found a need for many more double deckers, but in some places the use of standard height vehicles was prevented by low bridges, or by the height of the depot where they were needed. On the Ilkeston route, Straws Bridge, between West Hallam and Ilkeston provided such a constraint, whilst, similarly on the Burton route, Willington Bridge had the same effect. At Melbourne, the depot was too low to accommodate highbridge buses, and about eight lowbridge Regents were allocated there The greatest number were at Meadow Road, but there were also a couple at Shipley, five at Nottingham, and Loughborough had but a solitary example.

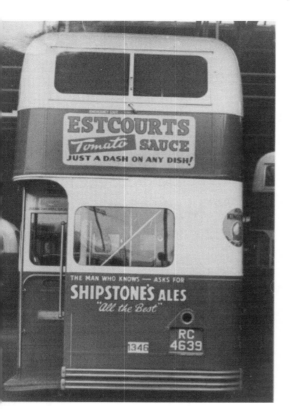

1351, RC 4648, formerly 1042, to the right, awaits a turn of duty on service 18 to Tutbury, whilst lower right, 1344, RC 4635, formerly 1029, heads in to The Morledge, at Derby. Both were rebodied in 1949, and Although post war pattern front wings were fitted, covering the chassis dumb irons, the pre war, short radiator was retained, but note that in the case of 1351, the blanking plate on the radiator extends deeper, giving an illusion of the later style.

Above, 1341, RC 4639, formerly 1033, was new in 1937, rebodied in 1948 and finally withdrawn from service in 1959. The white, or silver, number plate, with red painted numbers, indicates that it was allocated to Shipley depot. Note the single tail lamp above the registration plate, and the double bumper bar, which was later removed.

Highbridge AECs

Most of the remaining pre-war AECs received highbridge Willowbrook bodywork and retained their original numbers until nearly due for withdrawal, at which point they were renumbered 1162-8, some of the original numbers being required for incoming batches of new Leylands.

RC 4632, to the right, has been renumbered 1167, thus dating the photograph as around 1957/8. It, was withdrawn in 1958, being originally numbered 1026. Note the new, post war front wings, but retention of the original radiator on 1167.

1041, RC 4647, below, shown at Nottingham Huntingdon Street Bus Station, soon after return from Willowbrook in 1948.

Daimler COG5s

Twenty three further Daimler COG5s were rebodied during 1948, of which the majority, eighteen, received Brush H56R bodies, the remaining five being treated by Willowbrook.

The Brush bodies showed some resemblance to the builders final wartime design, which had been quite well proportioned and carefully detailed, so far as wartime constraints had allowed, features were carried through to post war production, the resulting bodies having a well balanced and agreeable appearance. In the top left picture, 1081, RC 7945, dating from 1940, leaves Huntingdon Street probably returning to Manvers Street depot. On the right, 1069, RC 7080, of 1939 awaits service to Wirksworth, from Derby. Both were finally withdrawn in 1958.

The Willowbrook bodies, had a much improved design, compared with the 1946 examples from the same supplier. The windows were now rubber gasket glazed in radiussed pans, the body tapered gently inwards towards the front, and the cab was now integrated more effectively into the body, whilst the infill panel behind the nearside front wing added a finishing touch to the appearance. 1063, RC 7074, was new in 1939, and was withdrawn from service in 1957. The bus had a good load when photographed at 4.20pm in a remarkably deserted Ripley Market Place - the shops are closed, so perhaps it was half day closing!

Final single deck rebodies

Amongst the last vehicles to be refurbished were the 1936 SOS DONs, originally with Brush B34F bodies, rebodied in 1949, and the 1937 AEC Regals, which ended the programme in 1950. and were previously fitted with Willowbrook or Duple bodies to the standard pre-war Trent design. Most were rebodied by Willowbrook.

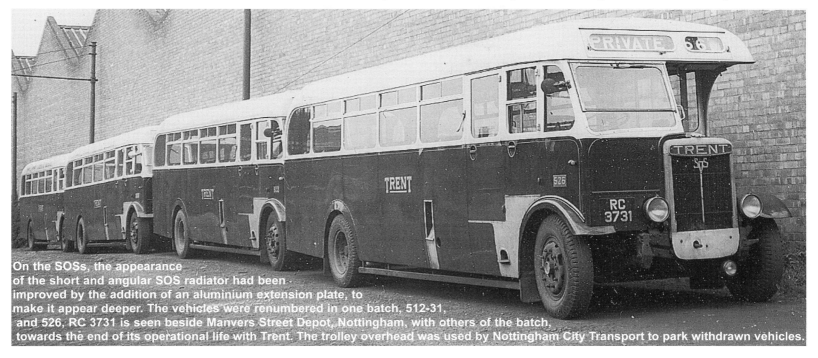

On the SOSs, the appearance of the short and angular SOS radiator had been improved by the addition of an aluminium extension plate, to make it appear deeper. The vehicles were renumbered in one batch, 512-31, and 526, RC 3731 is seen beside Manvers Street Depot, Nottingham, with others of the batch, towards the end of its operational life with Trent. The trolley overhead was used by Nottingham City Transport to park withdrawn vehicles.

The 1937 AEC Regals received new radiators and front wings similar to those fitted to post war models. With the new Willowbrook B35F bodies fitted in 1950 they looked virtually indistinguishable from the vehicles supplied new in 1948. The batch lasted in their new form until 1958. 700, RC 4601, was photographed at Buxton Market Place in August 1951.

Two fine AECs at work! In this September 1954 view, taken in York Street, Nottingham, draymen unload crates of Whitbread's ales from the Mammoth Major at the site of the former Nottingham Brewery Co, whilst the conductor hangs from the platform of Trent 1950 Regent III 1201, BRC 401, to reset the blind for the next journey to Mansfield. The 56 seat body on 1201 was almost the final development of Willowbrook's traditional form of double deck bodywork, and the last double deckers supplied to Trent until 1958. The area forming the backdrop to the photograph has long since disappeared to make way for new development, whilst the bus was withdrawn in 1964. Whitbread no longer owns any breweries, and doubtless, the Mammoth Major has also ended its days.

Post War AECs

During the period 1946-50, the Company took delivery of no less than 171 new vehicles, all on AEC chassis and with Willowbrook bodywork. In addition there were also six AEC chassis purchased which received pre-war coach bodies. The vehicles, particularly the double deckers, showed a development of Willowbrook's design from a rather crude looking wartime based design to an attractive, well detailed and finished design. Bodies to similar designs were also being concurrently fitted to the Company's refurbished pre-war chassis.

The first new chassis after the war were six AEC Regals, RC 8740-5. These received pre- war bodies originally fitted to Daimler COG5 chassis, retaining the same fleet numbers, 637-42. Unlike the majority of the AECs then in in the fleet, which had pre-selector gearboxes, the chassis had crash gearboxes, which set the standard for the fleet until 1950. 638, RC 8741, awaits private hire, express or excursion duty at Huntingdon Street, Nottingham.

The vehicles gave ten years service in the fleet, and were withdrawn in 1956, well into the underfloor engine era. By this time the eighteen years old bodies were looking extremely old fashioned, particularly by coach standards, but the appearance was not helped in this case by the loss of the front wheel nut ring. In the company of, amongst others, coaches of Black & White and Southdown, 641, RC 8744, takes a layover on some sunny summer excursion.

AEC did not produce passenger chassis during the war years, being required to concentrate on work for the military. However, Trent were obviously impressed by their pre-war AECs, for during the war years orders were placed for further examples for fulfillment after the end of hostilities. One of the first to arrive was 1120, RC 8918, photographed in October 1946 at Huntingdon Street, Nottingham. The vehicle carries the unrelieved BET light red livery adopted for a short time in the early post war period. In the background is the Barton Nottingham depot, nowadays used by a tyre company.

The Willowbrook H54R bodywork fitted to these vehicles represented a stage in Willowbrook's double deck bodywork development, for it was more refined than that shown on the first rebodied Daimlers, as illustrated on page 50, but lacked the rubber gasket glazing of the style of body shown on page 62. This 1957 view shows 1132, RC 9648, in the layover area at Derby Bus Station, in an area later modified to accommodate the Inner Ring Road.

New single deckers arrived in 1946 in the form of 34 AEC Regal IIs. These had Willowbrook B34F bodywork to a new design, although there was a clear affinity in terms of detailing to the manufacturer's double deck design. 744, RC 9010, was photographed at Uttoxeter Road, at the end of its operating life with Trent .

The new Regals had the familiar AEC 7.7 litre engine, coupled to a crash gearbox. They gave good service, those in original form lasting in the fleet until 1960, but by this time they were rather dated and low in capacity. 737, RC 9003 was photographed at Leek, some time in the mid fifties.

This rear view shows the centre rear emergency exit, which kept the capacity down by one seat, to 34, and meant that no luggage boot was provided. Later deliveries had an off side emergency exit, with 35 seats and a boot, and could be pressed into use on seaside express services, although this was unpopular with the public.

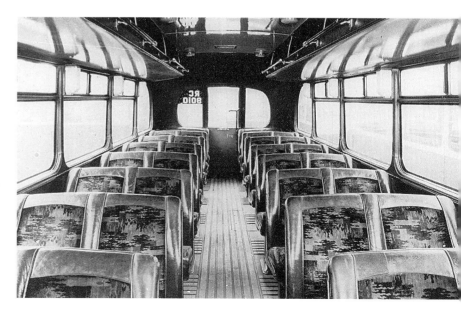

The interior view, shows brown leather trimmed seats, covered with moquette that incorporated brown, black, beige and orange in the pattern. Also visible is the registration number, illuminated at night by some of the interior lights.

New coaches delivered for 1948 were twelve of the new AEC Regal III models with Windover Huntingdon C33F coachwork of attractive appearance. Windover had been a builder of bespoke bodywork for high class motor cars but, in common with other companies, had entered the bus and coach market at a time of high demand after the war. Possibly for this reason they lacked experience, and the rear domes gave trouble, letting in water and requiring remedial work, including welding and additional support, out of season. Despite this, they gave a creditable twelve years service life, and one, 611, has survived into preservation. The style of dress of the tour participants in this view, taken when the vehicle was quite new and on a Scottish tour, gives us some reminder of how things used to be, rather formal and, perhaps, life at a slower pace.

Later in life, the rather heavy ivory and BET dark red livery gave way to a livery of mainly ivory, with just the wings and decorative tear drops in light red, which improved the appearance considerably. The gothic fleetname gave way to a polished aluminium version on a red backing, affixed in the middle, below the waistrail moulding. These, in fact, were copied from the Willowbrook bodied Royal Tigers delivered in 1953, and may have been made by Willowbrook. 606, ACH 436, right, sports the new livery, although with the original fleetname, on a tour to Lands End. Just a little informality is now evident in the dress style, but not much!

608, ACH 438, left, illustrates one characteristic that this batch of coaches introduced to the fleet. Fleetnumber plates were painted ivory, with the number painted in the depot colour code. This contrasted with buses, on which the background was painted in the appropriate colour, and the numbers usually left as polished metal.

A fine portrait shot of 762, RC 9668 right, one of the AEC Regal IIs with Willowbrook B35F bodywork delivered in 1948, taken when new at Huntingdon Street, Nottingham. Unlike the similar vehicles delivered in 1946, these had the emergency exit situated on the offside, directly behind the driver, allowing a one piece rear window, five seats across the back instead of four, and a luggage boot. This enabled the vehicles to be used on seaside express services on summer Saturdays. The vehicles also featured a heater, for which the equipment was built into the canopy.

Although the Regals proved highly satisfactory in service, their use on express services led to complaints from passengers. In 1958, when they were already ten years old but had run low mileage, twenty of the batch were modernised and lengthened to 30ft (9.144m). The chassis work was fairly minimal, amounting to some minor frame extensions at the back, and was done by Trent. Work to the body was more extensive, and the original builders, Willowbrook, converted it to full front, extended the rearmost bay, fitted new semi coach seating for 39 and generally refurbished the interior. The external appearance was completed with additional mouldings and a livery, clearly inspired by the 1954/5 Willowbrook bodied Tiger Cubs shown on page 73. The new fully fronted cab had a nearside door as well as the usual offside one, and this provided extra luggage accommodation, but the cabs became extremely warm in the summer. After a long run, drivers were apt to be wet through with sweat and, consequently, came to refer to the vehicles as "sweat boxes." 312, RC 9687, below, in June 1958, just after completion of the conversion.

The first vehicle treated, 757, RC 9663 below, had windows directly glazed with rubber gaskets, but the remaining conversions did not, as there was a need to reduce the conversion cost of £1475 per vehicle. 757 was renumbered 300, and a further 19 vehicles were converted, being renumbered 301-19. There was no change to the rear appearance, beyond the brightwork on the lower edge, and the flashing indicators. In this early sixties view, Derby Corporation is still running trolleybuses, Cornmarket has yet to be pedestrianised, and Barlow and Taylor's Department store, on the top right, is not yet the Derbyshire Building Society. Note also the police officer, on point duty by the front trolley, the dress style of the motorcyclist and, indeed the motor cycle itself.

A further twenty new AEC Regent IIs arrived for 1948. Again, these had Willowbrook bodywork, but incorporating the improved design features, similar to the final five rebodied Daimlers pictured earlier. There were ten each of lowbridge and highbridge models, and two of the former are illustrated above. The lower overall height, and resulting shallower upper deck panels, gave these vehicles better proportions than the highbridge version, shown below, resulting in a pleasing and stylish appearance. On the left is 1329, ACH661, the solitary lowbridge Regent allocated to Loughborough depot in the mid fifties. On the right, is a March 1952 view of 1325, ACH 657 off service at Derby Bus Station. These vehicles were withdrawn in 1963, giving a creditable fifteen years service life.

The ten highbridge examples had a similar specification and appearance, as illustrated by this view of 1153, ACH 643, taken at Nottingham Huntingdon Street Bus Station. The picture was probably taken in the late fifties, judging by the lack of lining on the red panels below the lower deck waist rail. Half of this batch also lasted until 1963, but others were withdrawn a year earlier.

For 1950, twenty new AEC Regal IIIs arrived with attractive Willowbrook DP33F bodywork. They were unique in having a Crossley syncromesh gearbox, compared with the crash or pre-selector units offered as standard by AEC, and this gave them a distinctive and easily recognisable sound. They were not popular with drivers, however, since the gear change was rather slow and obstructive, when compared with other types. The advent of underfloor engine vehicles, with higher seating capacity and modern looking full front, caused the vehicles to quickly become dated and they achieved a service life of only eleven years, being withdrawn in 1961. 103, BRC 303, was photographed at Alfreton in August, 1953.

In later years, as the vehicles were relegated to bus status, they lost the BET dark red paint within the streamline mouldings in favour of the standard light red, which spoilt the appearance somewhat. However, this did not prevent 101, BRC 301 being used on a private hire duty, probably from Alfreton, to which depot it was allocated. It was photographed in Manchester, closely followed by a Beardmore taxi - like AEC, another lost manufacturer. In a perhaps surprising move in 1960, two of the batch were painted in a reversed livery of cream with light red streamlining for an airport service.

The traditional AEC radiator always had an imposing and quality appearance, greatly enhanced when the shell was chromium plated, as on the Regent III and Regal III series. The twenty Regals shown above were accompanied in 1950 by ten Regent IIIs, also with Willowbrook bodywork, and also with the Crossley gearbox. By now, the Willowbrook double deck body had reached a quite refined appearance, and 1207, BRC 407 looks resplendent as it stands, when new in June 1950, at Huntingdon Street Bus Station, Nottingham. These vehicles achieved fourteen years service, being withdrawn in 1964.

The first new Leylands supplied to the Company (other than a solitary Tiger, inherited with the takeover of E Bramley's Prince of Wales service in 1930) were six PD2/3s with Leyland H56R bodies, 1220-5, CCH 620-5. It is said that they were a diverted order, as there was evidence on the platform bulkhead of a painted waistband beneath the Trent livery, but this has not been confirmed. Certainly, when the Board approved the purchase of these vehicles in September 1950, there had been no specific plans to purchase new vehicles for 1951, but the chassis numbers confirm that they were built in 1951, and Leyland records show no evidence of a diverted order. The crew confer at Mansfield Westgate, when 1225 had just entered service in April, 1951, before setting off for Nottingham.

Leyland - the new supplier.

Starting in 1951, Leyland Motors Ltd became the Company's exclusive chassis supplier for the period until 1959. Virtually all of Leyland's home market chassised models were supplied, and a considerable number of bodies also came from the Leyland works. This was a complete change of policy, the reason for which has not been found. Even in 1959, only a few AEC coach chassis were bought, and even after the Daimler Fleetline became the standard double deck chassis, all single deck and coach purchases came from Leyland, a situation which continued until Leyland achieved its dominant and near monopoly market position as British Leyland.

The ten Leyland Royal Tiger coaches received shortly after the PD2s had Leyland C41C coachwork of restrained but well proportioned appearance. The Royal Tiger, with the Leyland O.600 engine in horizontal form, was Leyland's first main stream underfloor engine chassis. It was heavy, returning relatively poor fuel consumption compared with earlier vehicles, and was soon superseded for the home market by lighter models. The weight also affected the performance of the vacuum brakes, which had a poor reputation, being subject to fading in frequent use. 206, CRC 516, right, was caught on a private hire duty, probably in mid-life, after the original semaphore trafficators had been replaced by flashing units.

The batch consisted of 200-9, CRC 510-9, starting a fresh series for coaches, and 201, above, was photographed at Huntingdon Street Bus Station, Nottingham, about to take up duty on the X2 Manchester service, the vehicles being used for this type of work and for private hire, not for the company's tour programme.

The batch was withdrawn in two stages in 1961/2, but in their closing years some received bus livery for use on peak hour stage carriage work, as demonstrated by 209, CRC 519, below, leaving Derby on service to Barrow on Trent.

The Titan PD2/3 chassis had the vertical Leyland O.600 9.6 litre engine, syncromesh gearbox and vacuum brakes, whilst the body was the latest development of Leyland's metal framed product, introduced in this form in 1935, but subject to progressive development. 1223, CCH 623, photographed when quite new, awaiting passengers on the Grantham service, joint with Lincolnshire, was renumbered 713 in 1962, and the batch was withdrawn in 1964.

The next batch, delivered in 1952 were on PD2/12 chassis, of the newly authorised 27ft length, giving an extra 1ft, carried what was virtually Leyland's final development of the metal framed body. All windows featured radiussed corners with rubber gasket glazing which, together with the replacement of the previous half drop windows by top sliding units, produced a modern and pleasing appearance. The full batch was 1226-35, CRC 826-35, which remained in service until 1964.

More PD2/12s arrived in 1953 and 1954, following the style of the 1952 vehicles. Those delivered in 1953 were 1236-50, DRC 936-50, and 1243 is shown here leaving Leicester St Margaret's for Loughborough on the 625 service, jointly operated with Midland Red. Most of these lasted until 1965, but two or three hung on until 1967. A final batch arrived in 1955, 1250-6, FRC 950-6, which were the last Leyland bodies built at Leyland, and these remained in service until 1965-67.

From 1953, electrically operated platform doors, controlled by the conductor from buttons on the platform, were fitted to the Leyland bodies on PD2/12 chassis. 1241, new in 1953 and showing Ashbourne allocation by its red and black number plate was photographed in Uttoxeter Market Place, probably around 1960.

The interior views below show the lower deck, left, and upper deck of the Leyland metal framed body at the end of its production run. Using tan interior trim, with mid brown leather seat coverings, they offered a solid and well finished feel for the last traditionally constructed double deckers in the fleet.

The Company's first underfloor engine, front entrance buses were ten Leyland Royal Tigers. The driver now sat with the passengers, separated only by a tubular barrier liftable for access, and this led, over a period, to an improvement in the appointments of the cab area, but the conductor was left with nowhere to stand when not collecting fares. However, there was the advantage that the driver could now supervise the entrance when the conductor was busy. 806, DCH 906 is parked in Huntingdon Street Bus Station at Nottingham in April, 1953, having run in from Sutton in Ashfield on service 84, taken over from Dutton's Unity Service in the thirties.

The Leyland B44F bodywork, with shallow roof contour and square front was rather severe. The waist line was rather high, due to the high build necessary to accommodate the underfloor engine, but the double line of polished aluminium moulding helped to break up the expanse, and the polished aluminum fleetname on the front added a decorative feature. Note the severe rake of the windscreen, introduced on the first generation of underfloor engine buses, which helped to minimise reflections from the internal lighting at night - a greater problem without a separate cab. The batch of vehicles, withdrawn in 1962, was numbered 800-9, DCH 900-9, and 801 awaits passengers at Derby for the short run to the village of Weston on Trent.

Six Royal Tiger touring coaches, delivered in 1953 had Willowbrook centre entrance 41 seat coachwork and were rather more flamboyant in external design than the Leyland bodied examples of 1951. Numbered 210-5, ECH 210-5, 214 is seen around 1960 at Thorpe Road Bus Station in Norwich, return to Nottingham from Great Yarmouth.

This superb and atmospheric portrait shot, posed somewhere in the Peak District, shows 210, the first of the batch when new. In later life the panels above the wheel arches, enclosed by the streamlined moulding incorporating the polished aluminium fleetname, were painted red and in 1962 the batch was renumbered 4-9, before withdrawal in 1963. Note the smart, almost military, attire of the driver and, just visible in the nearside front windscreen, the all important and eagerly sought after front seat giving the same view to the front as that of the driver. The antimacassar placed over each head rest gave that final touch to these well appointed vehicles. Pictorial badges, with a colourful animal portrait, as on the front of this vehicle, were an attractive feature of Leyland vehicles during the fifties. These were excellent vehicles, if rather heavy, but at the end of their service life, they were hired to British Railways for transporting track maintenance gangs. After subsequent sale by Trent, they were acquired by contractors Wimpey and A Monk for transporting site labour. A sorry end for such fine vehicles but, on the second hand market, their potential uses were very limited.

As described in the text, the industry had faced increasing costs since the war, especially for fuel, and was turning to lighter weight vehicles in an effort to combat this. Leyland introduced the Tiger Cub PSUC1/1 chassis in 1952, with a 5.76 litre horizontal O.350 underfloor engine, already used in considerable numbers as a vertical unit in the Comet goods chassis. The engine developed 90bhp, and was close coupled to a four speed constant mesh gearbox, the chassis having full air pressure brakes and lightweight axles with smaller wheels than the Royal Tiger, compared with which it was some two tons (1,968kg) lighter. Trent received twenty Tiger Cubs in 1954, the first ten, 810-19, FCH 10-19, having B44F bodywork by Saro (Saunders Roe Engineering and Shipbuilding Co, of Anglesey). This sixties view, left, shows 366, FCH 16, previously numbered 816, in The Morledge, Derby.

Saro were very active bus body builders at that time that these vehicles were delivered, although they went out of business soon afterwards and, despite their full name, they also built aircraft. These ten bodies were of aluminium construction and built to an almost "monocoque" form, using aircraft principals, to achieve their light weight. Indeed, an integral vehicle of similar appearance was built and supplied to Maidstone and District. They had some American influence in their appearance, but were attractive and well proportioned vehicles, as illustrated by 813, FCH 13, at Nottingham. When new, the cantrail panels of these vehicles were painted red.

The rear featured a centre emergency exit and rounded appearance. The internally illuminated numberplate proved vulnerable to damage, and was soon replaced by transfers in the top of the rear offside window, relying on the interior lights for night time illumination, some being wired in with the side lights for this purpose.

The second ten 1954 Tiger Cubs, 820-9, FCH 30-9, had B44F bodies by Weymann to their "Hermes" design. These, too, were of attractive and well proportioned appearance but, unlike the Saro bodies, were of steel framed construction. Most were allocated to Nottingham or Loughborough depots, and 828, FCH 28 was photographed at the Rushes, Loughborough, opposite the Trent depot, in April 1955. The red panels above the cant rail were a feature of these vehicles for some years, and often carried advertisements, but were painted ivory in later life. Note also the darker red wheel arches, which were painted in standard light red in later years. The batch remained in service until 1965, being renumbered 370-9 in 1962. The vehicle behind is one of the 1950 AEC Regal IIIs with Willowbrook DP33F bodywork.

Also a Loughborough based vehicle, although here photographed in Stockwell Gate, Mansfield, on excursion duties well away from its normal operating area, was 827, FCH 827. In the mid fifties experiments took place with a livery of red with a cream band, and evidence of the participation of this vehicle in those experiments is provided by the non standard moulding below the waistline and running through the Tiger Cub badge. The experiment did not find favour, and the vehicle reverted to standard livery.

The interior of the vehicles was based on green moquette with leather trim, featuring overhead luggage racks and seating for 44. These vehicles, and the Saro bodied examples, saw about thirteen years good service with Trent, but after sale, many worked longer with their new owners than with Trent!

In pre-motorway times, the Tiger Cub was also useful for the Company's express services, especially when fitted with an Eaton two-speed rear axle. This was electrically operated by a plunger switch on the gear lever, and gave cruising advantages, but could be difficult to use and become troublesome. The greater area of ivory in the livery distinguished the vehicles as something more than a bus, but less than a coach, leading the Company to refer to them as "semi-coaches". Ten, 130-9, GRC 130-9 received Weymann DP41F bodies, based on an outline derived from the "Hermes" bus body, but with a suitably modified front to make it look less bus like, and with an emergency exit amidships on the off-side, to allow an extra seat and a luggage boot at the back. 132, GRC 132, delivered in 1954, leaves Lower Moseley Street, Manchester in the early sixties for the return run to Derby on service X1, although a Nottingham allocated vehicle. Similar bodies were supplied to other BET companies, including neighbouring North Western, and to Aldershot & District, although in both cases on AEC Reliance chassis, and with different external moulding designs and other differences.

Whilst the vehicles were very suitable for use on express services, they could also be used on stage carriage services. 130, GRC 130 is seen here operating service 84 from Sutton in Ashfield and illustrates the original style of fleetname fitted to these vehicles, built into the mouldings and with polished aluminium lettering. Note the tiny fleetnumber plate, on the offside, just above the panel strap at the front. These were introduced from 1953, for coaches and dual-purpose vehicles only.

The interior featured seats with head rests to further the half way house impression, and overhead luggage racks, although the racks were also fitted on buses. This view shows the interior of the Weymann version.

As related in the text, a prototype dual purpose Tiger Cub, 120, with high-waisted Willowbrook 41 seat body was delivered to the Company towards the end of 1954. This was followed by a further 9, 121-9, GRC 121-9 in the first part of 1955, and later that year twelve more, 140-151, HRC 140-51 with similar bodywork arrived.

The Willowbrook concept was identical to that of the Weymann version and, again, other BET undertakings took similar bodies, including East Yorkshire, which had some rear entrance versions, also on Tiger Cub chassis. 151, HRC 151, sets down passengers in Mount Street, Nottingham, in March, 1956, having run in from Hucknall, to which depot it was allocated. Behind is one of Barton's noted BTS rebuilds - of Leyland chassis, with Barton "Viewmaster" body.

Amongst the new double deckers delivered in 1956 were further Leyland PD2/12s, 1257-66, JCH 257-6. The chassis were much as delivered in previous years but, rather than Leyland, these vehicles were bodied by Metro Cammell, to their Orion design, Like the Tiger Cubs illustrated previously, the Orion was usually a lightweight design, intended to reduce fuel consumption, although neighbouring Nottingham City Transport had a batch of 44, only some of which were light weight. It featured directly glazed windows, secured by rubber gasket, and single skin frameless front and rear dome construction to the upper deck, both features helping to reduce weight, but contributed to a slightly austere appearance. The front upper deck pillars were rather thick, due to the form of construction used and the skirt panels rather shallow, whilst the different window depths perhaps strike a slightly jarring note, although the deep windows on the lower deck were advantageous for standing passengers. Despite these features, the design, although widely criticised at the time, was not unattractive in terms of proportions and general outline, and has, in the authors view, stood the test of time when viewed from over forty years later. It certainly met the needs of the industry in those weight conscious times, and was widely bought by both BET Companies, and Municipal operators. Newly delivered 1260, JCH 263 storms Derby Road hill, closely followed by a pre-war Vauxhall car, and a Park Royal bodied AEC Regent III of Nottingham City Transport.

Six of the PD2s, 1352-7, JCH 352-7 had similar bodywork, but to low-bridge pattern, which resulted in equal depth windows, but untidy detailing around the cab and canopy area. Slightly deeper windows were fitted at the front of the upper deck due to the low headroom and to assist forward visibility for passengers sitting on the transverse four person bench seats, along the offside sunken gangway. 1354, JCH 1354, allocated to Nottingham for the Chesterfield service, which had low bridges at the Chesterfield end, was expertly photographed by Geoff Atkins at Mansfield, when new.

Nottingham depot had only a limited requirement for lowbridge buses, and by the time this photograph was taken, probably around 1960/1, 1354 had been transferred to Melbourne depot, which could not accommodate highbridge deckers. Note the red and white fleetnumber plate on the bonnet to confirm the allocation. This view in the now pedestrianised Derby Market Place provides another indication of the way things used to be, and Cantors furniture shop, in the background is nowadays a bar.

Further highbridge Orions followed in 1956, a very large order for 34 vehicles, these starting a new series with fleetnumbers 1000-34, KCH 100-34. The 1XXX series of numbers was by now rapidly becoming available as the pre-war Daimlers and AECs and utility Daimlers so numbered were leaving the fleet. By the time this photograph of KCH 103 turning from Albert Street into St Peters Street in Derby was taken, the vehicle had been renumbered from 1003 to 760 in the 1962 renumbering scheme.

The Tiger Cub chassis with two-speed rear axle was taken into the fleet for coaches, too, although what the clients thought of the rather coarse sounding O.350 engine is not recorded. The Burlingham Seagull coachwork fitted was, however, amongst the best available and the attractive design, not unlike the Willowbrook bodied Royal Tiger shown on page 69 in concept, but somehow better executed, was to become a classic of its day, still standing scrutiny. On one of its first jobs, in June 1955, new coach 218, GRC 218, takes on passengers for a Scottish Highlands Tour, outside Huntingdon House, Trent's Nottingham traffic and booking office, opposite Huntingdon Street Bus Station. Trent had an extremely good name in coach holidays, being one of a limited number of territorial companies to make a name for itself in this area of operation, which can be quite difficult. This continued until National Bus Company days when the holidays were eventually centralised under new arrangements to be described in a subsequent volume.

The vehicles came in two batches, 216-221, GRC216-21, delivered in 1955, as illustrated on this page, and 222-8, KCH 222-8, delivered in 1957, shown opposite. The 1955 batch were the first coaches with front entrance, and 218, GRC 218 basks in the sunshine on a summer excursion, probably in 1959 or 1960. By now, the vehicle has acquired a front fleetnumber plate and these were introduced around 1958, being of normal size, rather than the very small size used for coaches and dual-purpose vehicles since 1953.

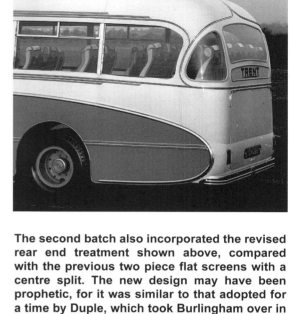

The second batch also incorporated the revised rear end treatment shown above, compared with the previous two piece flat screens with a centre split. The new design may have been prophetic, for it was similar to that adopted for a time by Duple, which took Burlingham over in 1958. Opinions of the changed design were divided but, in the author's view, it helped to keep the Seagull up to date.

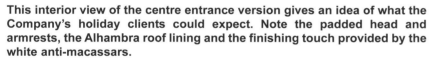

This interior view of the centre entrance version gives an idea of what the Company's holiday clients could expect. Note the padded head and armrests, the Alhambra roof lining and the finishing touch provided by the white anti-macassars.

This September 1958 view of 228, KCH 228, of the second batch provides an interesting contrast with the lower view on the opposite page. the Company reverted to the centre entrance, and it can be speculated that this was as a result of complaints about the loss of the seat next to the driver, but there may have been other reasons. However, despite the similarity of the design to the the previous batch, this change had a quite noticeable effect on the lower frontal design, which could be more curvaceous, without the need to accommodate the entrance. A further change was to flat windscreen glass, although still accommodated in a curved frontal profile.

The 1958 Leyland PD3/4s with Willowbrook H73RD bodywork were magnificent vehicles. They were similar in construction to the Metro-Cammell Orions delivered on PD2 chassis over the previous two years, but they were better proportioned, helped by the even window depth on both decks and the inward taper towards the roof. They had a capacious cab and were quite pleasant to drive, by the standards of the day, emitting a deep, almost sporting exhaust note. Attractive vehicles all round, and amongst the author's favourites. The vehicles were delivered without trafficators, but these were retro-fitted, to the side and rear, almost immediately. In later life, the nearside destination box was painted or paneled over. Photographer Roy Marshall recorded 1052, LRC 452, at Huntingdon Street, Nottingham, when new.

During 1964, all the PD3s, except the original experimental vehicle, 404 (formerly 1038), were fitted with fluorescent internal lighting. More obvious externally was the change of the destination box to a style similar to that used by Ribble, and this was probably inspired by the new Chief Engineer, Mr V J Owen, who had previously been at Ribble. 410, LRC 444, previously 1044, was photographed on Nottingham's Maid Marian Way, seemingly at a stage of partial construction, judging by the lack of road markings.

Interior views of the upper and lower deck. On the upper deck, three extra seats were obtained by cantilevering the floor over the lower deck platform, something which had not previously featured in the Trent fleet. Seat covering was brown leathercloth, and a continuous strip bell ran along the lower deck ceiling, another new feature for Trent.

The first new vehicles to arrive in 1959, were 152-61, NRC 152-61, ten Leyland Tiger Cub PSUC1/2 models with Willowbrook DP41F bodywork, introducing a standard BET design to the fleet for the first time since the early Tilling Stevens. The chassis were the latest version of the Tiger Cub, featuring an Albion five-speed constant mesh gearbox, in place of the four speed Leyland unit, previously used, and the five speeds meant that the two-speed axle was no longer considered necessary. The gearbox had a noticeable whine, when compared with the previous models, due to the straight cut, rather than helical, gears, and was coupled to a larger O.375 engine of 6.17 litre capacity. The bodywork was to a newly introduced BET design, featuring an upright front and was rather plain, but generally well proportioned. The design was supplied to many operators, including those in the independent and municipal sectors, as well as BET subsidiaries, by a wide variety of manufacturers, as either a bus or dual-purpose vehicle. 152, seen at Nottingham, Mount Street Bus Station in 19xx was the regular performer for several years on Trent's journeys on the Nottingham-Derby Express service, X42, operated jointly with Barton.

158, NRC 158 in Wharncliffe Road, Ilkeston, operates a journey to Manchester one summer Saturday. The collars on the front waistband are to hold a removable plastic "EXPRESS SERVICE" sign of the type shown on 152, in the photograph above. These were used for a few years in the sixties.The livery was rather plain for a dual-purpose vehicle, adding only the ivory waistband and aluminium mouldings to the standard single deck bus livery. The fount used for the fleetname was to a style identical with that adopted by several BET companies for dual-purpose vehicles for a time. However, it was to prove short-lived, being replaced by the then current standard design at first or second repaint.The vehicles had a short service life of only nine years, being withdrawn in 1968, and after the 1964 summer season, were downgraded to B41F, and renumbered 350-9.

152 was one of the vehicles used for the first fluorescent lighting experiments, and this view shows the new lighting in operation, the plates covering the apertures for the original tungsten lighting being visible on the underside of the luggage racks. Whilst the interior was of modern appearance, making extensive use of plastic laminates, the seats look somewhat spartan for dual purpose vehicle - compare with those in the Weymann bodied Tiger Cubs of 1955, shown on page 73.

A return to AEC for touring coaches

Five new coaches, 229-33, RRC 229-33 arrived in 1960, and these marked an interesting change of policy, for they had AEC Reliance chassis, rather than the Leyland Tiger Cub that had been favoured in recent years. It will be recalled that the fleet of E Naylor & Sons had been taken over in 1956, and this had included two AEC Reliances, 646/7. The performance of these vehicles had impressed Trent considerably, with the result that the next order for coaches was placed with AEC.

The Leyland O.350/O.400 engine fitted to the Tiger Cub had a rather harsh sound, whereas the AEC engine sounded softer, and was thus more appropriate for coach use, but the general performance of the AEC was also felt to be superior for touring work, despite some tendency of the AH470 engine to overheat and blow cylinder head gaskets. This was a characteristic of the Reliance not fully overcome until much later models were fitted with the AH760 engine and a large header tank at higher level. The bodies on these vehicles were by Weymann, to their Fanfare design with front entrance and 37 seats, although this was increased to 41 in later years.

Weymann had traditionally been more associated with buses rather than coaches, but had produced the slightly flamboyant Fanfare design, which found some favour, mainly amongst BET operators, although others were also supplied. These two views show 229, RRC 229 (upper) and 230, RRC 230 (lower), undertaking private hire duties.

New coach deliveries for 1963 included four more Reliances, but with Harrington Cavalier C37F coachwork. At the same time as this order was being fulfilled, the chassis of 33 (formerly 233) was re-bodied, having been involved in a serious accident which badly damaged the original Weymann Fanfare body. Although repairable, the severity of the damage was such that, with the body order in hand for new coaches, it was decided that a new body was the better option, particularly as the Fanfare design had, in the meantime, become obsolete. 33, RRC 233, at Derby, after re-bodying.

The bus that changed the face of the industry. Forever. By the end of 1959, the first Leyland Atlanteans, twenty-two in number, had been delivered and entered service, these being PDR1/1 models, eleven, 1056-66, ORC 656-66, with Metro Cammell H78F bodies, of the type shown here, and a further eleven with low height Weymann H73F bodies. 1066, ORC 6xx was photographed fresh from the bodybuilders, leaving Huntingdon Street, Nottingham. Note, in addition to the wide range of innovations, the new pattern of destination box, a standardised single panel with masking to suit individual company requirements, and the use of numerals of much greater size than previously.

The Atlantean chassis had the Leyland O.600 engine, familiar from the Titan, but mounted transversely at the rear and driving through a four speed semi-automatic epicyclic gearbox and an angle drive with short propeller shaft to the rear axle. The gearbox was controlled electro-pneumatically, with a small electric lever on a binnacle beneath the steering wheel operating air controls on the gearbox. This system was later to become widespread, but was the first use of this system in the fleet and was given the brand name Pneumo-cyclic by Leyland. It made the driving task considerably easier, but operation of the gearchange was extremely easy, and could be abused if drivers failed to make a pause in neutral between gears, to avoid causing excessive wear on the brake bands in the gearbox, and ensure a jerk free change.

The Atlantean drive line was accommodated under a one piece cowling at the back of the vehicle, made of reinforced fibreglass and hinged along the top to provide easy access, but giving a rather odd appearance to the rear end. Leyland claimed that the unit was so accessible that the entire power pack could be exchanged in " a matter of minutes". The provision of a destination box on the back was a feature not seen on Trent vehicles since the pre-war forward entrance Daimlers and AECs. They fell out of use after a year or two and were paneled over.

Eleven of the lowbridge version, 1358-68, ORC 758-68, with Weymann H73F bodies were also received in 1959. the bodywork on both versions was derived from the Orion body, previously supplied on Titan chassis, but suffered in appearance due to the depth of upper deck paneling, aggravated by the style of painting adopted by the bodybuilders. 1365, ORC 765, stands at Ilkeston Market Place in March, 1960, alongside a pair of interesting Barton vehicles.

RAISED SEATS, WITH SUNKEN GANGWAY ALONGSIDE

Trent subsequently modified the style of painting, to good effect on the low bridge examples, as demonstrated by ORC 760, renumbered 602, but originally 1360 when new. This view, taken at Burton on Trent in May 1971, also shows the temple position adopted for the fleetname, and the relocation of the front registration plate above the windscreen, both to minimise the cost of accident repairs.

The low height version of the Atlantean was a half way house between the normal and lowbridge layouts, as these views of the interior upper and lower decks attempt to illustrate. The front of the lower saloon had a flat low floor, but in order to keep the cost of the complete vehicle as low as possible, a conventional straight rear axle was used, rather than the drop centre type as had been originally used on the prototype. This required a step up in front of the axle to a floor at higher level in the lower deck, whilst the upper deck had the rear section over this step arranged in the traditional lowbridge fashion with bench seats and a sunken gangway, and the front part was to a conventional layout. Very much a compromise, but Leyland had been keen to get the cost of the Atlantean chassis closer to that of the Titan.

STEP

Traditionally, the Leeds based Charles H Roe concern had a reputation for elegant and well proportioned bodywork, but Trent had received only a few utility Roe bodies during the war. In 1960, some 19 Roe bodied Leyland Atlanteans were delivered during the year, in two batches. These were, 1067-89, RRC 67-89, and, later in the year, 1090-95, TCH 90-5, all with Roe H78F bodies. The body was steel framed and based on a design developed at the behest of BET by parent company Park Royal for the AEC Bridgemaster. With their angular proportions, large expanse of paneling between decks, high upper deck window line and almost vertical sides, the vehicles had a rather ungainly appearance, which left much to be desired. In service, the bodies tended to drop around the entrance area, but they gave a full service life of twelve years, many going thereafter for service in Hong Kong. On the left, 435, RRC72, formerly 1072, is at Alfreton, and on the right 1070, RRC 70 awaits passengers at Derby. The "U" sticker in the windscreen of 1070 carries a notice to the driver on the reverse stating that the vehicle must be garaged in Uttoxeter New Road depot that night. Similar stickers, marked "M" gave a similar message in respect of Meadow Road depot.

The last Atlanteans for Trent for many years, and the last of the PDR1 version, were ten, 462-71, 62-71 ACH, with Weymann bodywork, the appearance of which was a slight improvement over those supplied by Roe. The left hand picture shows 463, 63 ACH, at Nottingham, whilst that on the right shows 468, 68 ACH at Loughborough Bus Station. Note the illuminated advertisement panel, fitted from new.

The AEC Reliance continued to find success with the Company for coach use, and four more were delivered in 1961, with Burlingham Seagull 70 bodies, shown on the page opposite, followed by a further four in 1962 with the Harrington Cavalier body, shown on this page. After these were delivered, the Company reverted to Leyland coaches, specifying the 36ft (10.97m) Leyland Leopard, when the maximum permitted box dimensions were increased. This was, perhaps, surprising, since the longer versions of the Reliance enjoyed a high level of sales success and were, in the authors view, rather more refined than the Leopard, in terms of engine noise, although the latter proved to be extremely reliable in long term service.

The Burlingham body was called the Seagull 70, doubtless wishing to capitalise on the success of its predecessor, to which it bore no resemblance. Interestingly, its general concept was quite similar to that of the Harrington Cavalier shown on this page, but Harrington managed to make their body crisper and more effective. The Cavalier was sold widely within the BET Group, but also found favour with a number of independent operators. Like the original Burlingham Seagull, it became a classic design of its time. The Burlinghams, 39-42, VCH 239-42 lasted until 1968, whilst the Harringtons, 43-6, YRC 43-6 were withdrawn in 1970.

On the opposite page, 41, VCH 241 was photographed at Nottingham, Huntingdon Street, whilst in the upper photograph, 40 was recorded operating a private hire.

On this page, in the upper photograph 43, YRC 43 was photographed at London's Earls Court. In the lower photograph, 44, YRC 44 was photographed at Blackpool in August 1962, awaiting return to Derby on the Summer extension from Manchester of service X1.

A large number of Tiger Cubs entered service in 1961, carrying both bus and dual purpose bodies by Willowbrook, to the standard BET pattern, which first entered the fleet in 1959. The buses seated 44, on the PSUC1/1 chassis and were numbered 830-44, VCH 830-44, following on from the Weymann Tiger Cubs of 1954. They had a good length of service life, remaining in the fleet until 1975/6.
In October, 1961, 843, VCH 843, was photographed outside Nottingham's Victoria Station, built by the Great Central Railway, in the area later taken up for the Victoria Centre, but adjacent to the clock tower, which still remains.

The driver signals to make a right turn from The Morledge into Platform 1 of Derby's Central Bus Station, as 834, VCH 834 carries just a few passengers in from Loughborough on the infrequent 36 service, probably sometime around 4.15pm, one afternoon. The area forming the backdrop to this photograph, known as Cock Pit Hill was demolished to make way for the Eagle Centre in 1978.

The dual-purpose Tiger Cubs, mounted on Tiger Cub PSUC1/2 chassis, with provision for a luggage boot, had DP41F bodywork to the same standard BET outline, but featuring the stylish moulding scheme shown, and additional decorative brightwork on the front panel. These vehicles saw extensive use on the Company's network of Summer express services, but their service life was fairly short, being withdrawn in 1970-1. Even before that date, they had been found to be surplus to Trent requirements, being sent on hire to former BET subsidiaries, including PMT, North Western and, as this example, Yorkshire Traction. 172, VCH 172, photographed in May, 1969, in Barnsley, on hire to "Tracky", as the latter company was sometimes known. There was less requirement for this type of vehicle in the winter months, and some would be delicenced and stored for the winter. However, at Christmas time, seats would be removed, and some would be hired to the Post Office for use on mail deliveries. About twelve were used in this way, but eventually this came to an end due to changes in the law relating to use as heavy goods vehicles. There were other problems, though, because manoeuvrability in small residential streets was a major problem and, occasionally, Trent engineering staff would be called upon to rescue the situation!

Twenty similar vehicles delivered in the following year, 1962, were numbered 177-96, YRC 177-96), but had the first bodies supplied to Trent by Alexander of Falkirk, Scotland. Previously supplying mainly to operators in its native Scotland, Alexander had begun to enjoy success south of the border, receiving some significant BET Group orders. The vehicles were not to Alexander design, but to the standard BET pattern, showing only minor differences in appearance from the Willowbrook bodies already supplied. A ready identification feature was the deep panel for the destination box, but a key difference from the Willowbrook bodies was the lack of opening vents in the side windows. Internal ventilation in hot weather was provided by vents in the roof, but the result was not entirely satisfactory. 183, YRC 183, at Lower Mosley Street, Manchester.

The Daimler marque made a significant return to the fleet in 1963, with the arrival of ten Fleetline CRG6 models. The Northern Counties H77F low height body, avoided the use of an upper deck sunken gangway, made possible by the Daimler drive line, which incorporated a unique form of concentric drive shaft, and a dropped centre rear axle. The Northern Counties body was well proportioned and carefully detailed, marking a significant improvement in appearance over the products recently supplied to the fleet by Roe and the MCW organisation. The 10.6 litre Gardner 6LX engine, with its legendary fuel consumption, was coupled to a semi automatic "Daimatic" gearbox, built under licence from Self Changing Gears, by then a Leyland subsidiary. The vehicles proved highly satisfactory, and many more Fleetlines entered the fleet at the expense of the Leyland Atlantean. 624, 624 CCH was new when leaving Derby for Ilkeston in some very wet weather.

The Daimler marque returns

Due to their low height, the new Fleetlines were used extensively on routes with a lowbridge requirement, including Burton, Ilkeston and Melbourne, where the low height of the depot imposed the requirement for low bridge vehicles for service 19. Careful detailing was a characteristic of the Northern Counties bodywork, and this included recessed window pans, paint lines tailored to the design features of the body, and panel details which appeared to have been thought out, rather than to have occurred. Despite some problems with the body construction, the vehicles remained in service until 1978, apart from two destroyed by fire in 1976. 618, 618 CCH was photographed at Derby in April, 1963.

A characteristic of the Northern Counties body was the provision of engine shrouds to disguise the recess required to allow the engine cover to open for access, as shown by 617, when new, on the left, and provision of the shrouds made a noticeable improvement to the the side profile of the vehicles, compared with the previous Atlanteans. However, some maintenance operations required the whole engine cover to be lifted, necessitating removal of the shrouds, and this was an additional complication. By the end of 1966, the shrouds had been permanently removed, as shown by 624, in May 1969, on the right, heading towards Derby and passing under Straws Bridge between Ilkeston and West Hallam, which for many years required the use of low bridge buses, and for which the low height Fleetlines were ideal.

The first 36ft long vehicles

With effect from July 1961,the overall box dimensions for buses had been increased to 36ft long by 8' 2½"wide (10.98m by 2.5m) and the Company soon placed an order for twenty four vehicles to the new dimensions. These materialised in 1963 as Leyland Leopards with Willowbrook DP51F bodywork of attractive appearance, 200-23, 200-23 CCH. The Leopard had originally been introduced in 1959 as a heavier duty version of the Tiger Cub with the Leyland O.600 in place of the O.350. It had been re-engineered to the new length, with larger wheels and with the front axle redesigned to ensure that the turning circle did not exceed that of the 30' vehicles. In this form, and with subsequent developments, the Leopard proved extremely reliable, and was to have a very long career, remaining in production until 1982. The Willowbrook bodywork was derived from that fitted previously to Tiger Cub chassis, but featured longer bays. The new front with double curvature two piece windscreen, was developed to BET specification and designed to minimise internal reflections, whilst the extended front roof line with slight peak effect to incorporate the destination box, gave a modern appearance, in tune with current styling trends. The livery featured additional areas of ivory, and the front moulding scheme was designed by, and unique to, Trent. They were attractive vehicles and achieved along service life, most lasting until 1978. They were used initially on front line express services, but were also suitable for a wide range of other duties, and 218, 218 CCH is shown in the upper picture on the medium distance service to Buxton, whilst 223, 223 CCH is shown operating a private hire or day excursion. Following the change to spray painting, the livery was altered, first by removal of the cream skirt, and later to a style similar to that used on the Alexander Y type bodies, which was easier to mask for painting.

The longer Leopard also proved eminently suitable as a coach, especially when fitted with the Plaxton Panorama body illustrated here. This had been introduced in 1959, originally in 30ft length, and its various features had moved coach styling significantly forward. These styling features included the widely spaced pillars, large windows, extensive use of GRP moulded front and rear panels enabling a sculptured form of styling, and the simplified brightwork scheme, all of which were used to even better effect with the additional length. The chassis, of the PSU3/3RT type, featured two speed axles and a four speed synchromesh gearbox, coupled to the horizontal O.600 engine. Three such vehicles, 1-3, were delivered near the end of 1963, originally carrying their already allocated registrations ACH 1-3B for first use in 1964. However, two were required to be licenced for 1963 Christmas tours and so all three received 1963 registrations 121-3 FCH. At this time, Local Authorities, which then carried responsibility for vehicle registration matters, were phasing in the new letter suffix system. The County Borough of Derby was changing from 1st January 1964, and hence the need to obtain different registration numbers. 1, 121 FCH is illustrated at Blackpool, operating the summer Saturday extension of the Manchester service. The lower photograph is undated, but the upper photograph was taken in July, 1964, when the vehicle was just six months old.

These two photographs illustrate to good effect the restrained but attractive lines of the Alexander Y type body. The eight supplied to Trent in 1964, 224-31, ACH 224-31B, were mounted on Leyland Leopard PSU3/1RT chassis, with two speed rear axles for long distance use. This was at a time when the Motorway network was being greatly expanded and announcements of extensions could regularly be heard on radio and seen on television. The Y type design had originally been developed for the Scottish Bus Group, which took many for its subsidiaries in coach, bus and dual purpose form, but it was also taken up by a wide range of BET Group companies, mainly for express use. The area of red was later increased to include the skirt area, up to the polished moulding, as shown on the cover. Derby power station in Full Street was still evident by its chimneys in this June 1964 view of 224, taken when the vehicle was nearly new.

Although the Y type bodies supplied to Trent had what were essentially coach appointments - high backed seats, internal forced air ventilation via individual outlets on the parcel racks above each seat, and panoramic windows, Trent numbered the vehicles in the dual-purpose series, putting them to use on express and stage carriage services. The front and rear windscreens were of identical form to those used on the lower and upper deck front of the Alexander bodies supplied to Trent on Daimler Fleetline chassis. The area of red in the livery was later increased to include the skirt area, below the polished moulding, as shown on the cover. These vehicles remained in service until 1978, and were ultimately equipped for one-person operation. 231 in seemingly dirty weather conditions in July 1966, waiting to leave Nottingham Huntingdon Street behind a Hall Bros Harrington bodied Leyland Leopard, soon to be acquired by Barton

New service buses delivered for 1964 were fifteen maximum length Leopards with Marshall B53F bodies, 300-15, ACH 300-15B. Marshall had entered the bus body market following its takeover of Mulliner of Birmingham, and had become a quite significant supplier to the BET Group. A rather work worn 300, ACH 300B, was photographed at Mansfield Westgate depot in April, 1972, by which time it had been equipped for one person operation, as shown by the "Pay as You Enter, Please have exact Fare" signs on the front and nearside. For this purpose, they had operated with the seating capacity reduced to 45, during 1968-69, since Trade Union agreements provided for one person operation only up to 45 seats. When new, the vehicles had an additional blind for intermediate destinations, but these were later removed.

The bodies were similar in outline to the dual purpose Leopards supplied by by Willowbrook in the previous year, but as this official view of 300 when new shows, the rear dome was identical with that at the front, and there was a double curvature rear window of similar form to the front windscreen, although shallower in depth to match the side windows. Overall, a very tidy design. The rear dome, which was now upright, was available for advertising, and put to use by the company with the "Take it Easy - Take a Bus" slogan. These vehicles remained in service until 1979/80, except for 303, which was destroyed by fire in 1976.

1964 marked a return to Leyland for tour coaches, when five Leopard L2 models with Harrington Grenadier C40F bodies were delivered. Longer side windows, deeper windscreen and a revised front panel gave the Grenadier further development of the highly successful Cavalier design. The L2 Leopard was the original version, as previously mentioned, and essentially a Tiger Cub chassis with the O.600 engine in place of the O.350, giving somewhat more power, and considerably greater torque. 58, ACH 58B is about to take a tour to Devon and Cornwall.

This view illustrates the rear end treatment of these vehicles, showing the sculptured form of styling, large curved rear windscreen and the internally illuminated sign written name panel, for so long a feature of coaches, but which has nowadays fallen from favour, largely due to the influence of mainland European designs, which did not include such a feature.

Four 36ft long Leyland Leopards with Plaxton C49F bodies, 4-7, ECH 4-7C were delivered in 1965. The chassis incorporated air suspension for the first time, designed to provide a smoother, better balanced ride. Unfortunately, although air suspension is standard on the majority of bus and coach chassis today, it was not considered entirely successful at that time, and several years were to pass before further air suspended vehicles entered the fleet. The 49 seat Plaxton bodywork, was an update of the successful Panorama design which, although having a simple, straight waistline, seemed to loose something with the fussiness of the additional brightwork, and the visual separation of the front bay from the remainder. Coach 7, ECH 7C, at Nottingham, when nearly new.

The interior appointments included the first application in the fleet of the new forced air ventilation, the individually controllable outlets for which are visible on the underside of the luggage racks. The air was taken in via scoops on the roofline, visible above the second pillar in the adjacent photograph. Seats were covered with a plastics material which, whilst looking like leather, was found to be hot in the summer and cold in winter, leading to complaints.

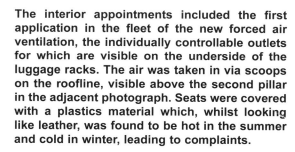

Other coaches for 1965 were something of a surprise, being six Bedford SB5s with Duple Bella Vega C41F bodies, 70-5, ECH 70-5C, for private hire and day excursion work. Replacing a cancelled order for five Leopard L1 chassis, they were something quite new to Trent, being a lightweight model of the type supplied to independent operators, and the first of the make ever operated. The chassis had a front mounted vertical Bedford 5.4 litre engine, coupled to a Turner syncromesh gearbox, and servo-assisted hydraulic brakes. 71, ECH 71C, at Derby Market Place in August 1965, when new. All six were withdrawn in 1971, but they had offered the opportunity to have an up to date appearance, at lower first cost, justifying earlier disposal.

Eight Tiger Cubs arrived in 1965 with Alexander Y type bodies, similar in every respect to those on Leopard chassis delivered the year previously. The chassis had the higher capacity O.400 engine, which with a revised fuel pump developed 125bhp, considered ample at the time, for the size of the vehicle. They remained in service until 1978/9, although some had by then been relegated to bus status, with appropriate livery, but retaining their original numbers. As described in the text, Trent had taken on responsibility for local control of United Counties' Nottingham-London service, and this included the provision of duplicates. In this April 1966 view, 104, HRC 104C, carries an "On Hire to United Counties" windscreen label, and the driver hurries along with his passenger chart, about to "dupe" on service MX5, as far as Northampton, although Trent would often run through to London.

Further double deckers delivered for 1965 were ten Daimler Fleetlines with Alexander H78F bodies, 472-81, ECH 472-81C. The Alexander bodies were to a design that was originally developed for Glasgow Corporation, and marked a move away from the box like appearance of bodywork that had been fitted to early rear engine double deck chassis. This was partly due to the use of curved glass windscreens that were identical to those used on the front and rear of the Y type coach body, shown opposite. However, the heavily rounded roof contours were apt to give the vehicles a rather tall appearance when viewed from the front. 478 was photographed in June 1965.

This official view of 472 shows that, unlike Northern Counties on the 1963 Fleetlines, Alexander made no attempt to disguise the engine cover, although there was a carefully designed profile to the side valances behind the lower deck windows, and, to some extent this made the engine appear like a bolt on extra. However, the vehicles made a good impression, for there were to be many more Alexander bodies ordered for the fleet. Most of the batch lasted until 1979/80, and were renumbered latterly into a 9xx series, to make way for new vehicles.

For 1985, Willowbrook offered to supply ten bodies like the Alexander Y type, and this was their interpretation! Compare this vehicle with those shown on page 94 and note the identical livery style, similar length side windows, twin head and fog lights mounted either side of a rectangular grille, and the single line destination box. However, these Willowbrook DP49F bodies were based on the standard BET pattern, which was rather more bus like than the Y type design. 232-41, ECH 232-41C, delivered in 1965 were intended to fulfill a similar function to the eight Alexander bodied Leopards of 1964 and had the same chassis specification, but, presumably, Willowbrook offered a better price or delivery date than Alexander. 232, ECH 232C was photographed at Blackpool in July, 1965, when nearly new. Note the X60 service number, used for the Ribble/North Western joint service between Blackpool and Manchester.

The general specification of the body of the vehicle shown above included fluorescent lighting, plastic laminate lining panels and forced air ventilation. They had a similar type of seat to those used in the 24 Willowbrook Leopards, of 1963, as shown below, but with the capacity reduced by two, for improved comfort.

There were also a further ten other Leopards, 242-51, ECH 242-51C, with broadly similar BET style Willowbrook bodies, although these had shorter side windows, different livery and, at the front, a full depth destination box and single headlights. They also had a seating capacity of 51 and no forced air ventilation, relying instead solely on the opening roof vents, and were generally similar to the 1963 Willowbrook bodied Leopards. They were originally to have been bodied by Weymann, but the order was diverted to Willowbrook, at some extra cost, due to a prolonged strike at Weymann, which ultimately resulted in the factory being closed. All twenty of the 1965 vehicles had a curved rear windscreen, with a rounded, rather than peaked, dome, as shown below.

The ten bodies ordered from Weymann materialised in 1966, but were built by the sister company, Metro-Cammell, better known for double deck bodywork at that time,but the Weymann factory at Addlestone had, by now closed down, with outstanding orders transferred to Metro-Cammell, then at Elmdon, near Birmingham. The 51 seat bodywork was to the by now standard BET design, and featuring the moulding scheme originally used on Willowbrook bodies in 1962. The grille beneath the windscreen was for a heating and ventilating system which was not entirely trouble free. The chassis was the Leyland Leopard PSU3/3R, 252-61, JRC 252-61D and, as with other, similar vehicles, they were used extensively on stage carriage and Summer express services. This portrait shot at Nottingham Huntingdon Street shows 261, JRC 261D, soon after delivery.

A further ten Alexander bodied Fleetlines arrived in 1966, 482-91, HRC 482-91D, very much as the previous year's delivery, although seating 77, rather than 78. As mentioned in the text, the Company had, during the cost cutting fifties and sixties, resorted to mechanical methods and other cost reduction measures wherever they could. In common with other operators, mechanical bus washing had been an early candidate for mechanisation, and after trying different types, including the "Essex" washer, a frame of brushes, surrounding the vehicle and passing up and down the sides, had settled on the vertical type which allowed the vehicle to be driven through. 488, receives a clean up after service to Wirksworth.

There were also just three Leyland Leopard L2 coaches delivered in 1966, 60-2, JCH 60-2D with Plaxton Panorama C40F coachwork. These were for the Company's holiday programme. and 61 was seen on just that type of work in Aberdeen's Union Street. The vehicles remained in the fleet until 1977. Further similar vehicles were delivered the following year.

Careful inspection reveals some longer window bays on a second 1967 batch of four coaches, which were PSU3/4R Leopards, delivered after the August registration change and receiving registrations PRC 208-11F with fleet numbers 8-11. The same Plaxton Panorama coachwork had seats for 49. Puddles and steamy windows were the order of the day on this excursion, as the driver chivvies his passengers to reboard the coach for the next stage of their trip.

The Bedford SB5s delivered in 1965 having proved satisfactory for their intended purpose, a further six Bedfords arrived in 1965. This time, however, they were of the SB's intended successor, the VAM5, first announced to the market in 1965. At a little over 32ft (9.75m), they were some 2ft (610m) longer than the SBs, and featured a set back front axle, which made versions with bus bodywork more suitable for one person operation. The Bedford 330 cu in engine was front mounted, as on the SB, and coupled to a Turner gearbox. The batch of vehicles was 76-81, MRC 576-81E, and 77 was caught by the camera doing what it was bought for - operating a private hire, seemingly to a popular place with a coach park.

A passenger impression of the interior of the Duple Viceroy 41 seat coachwork fitted to the Bedford VAMs. The entrance ahead of the front axle helped to make the vehicles indistinguishable to the untrained eye from vehicles on heavyweight chassis such as AEC or Leyland, and, whilst the Bedford engine was not the quietest, those sitting at the back would have been well away from the sound, and doubtless had a comfortable journey, with Bedford's generally agreeable ride qualities. Note the net overhead luggage racks and the lack of forced air vents, top sliding windows being provided for ventilation. The vehicles remained in service until 1972.

The Naylor fleet used a red and cream livery and operated a service in competition with Trent between Mansfield and Alfreton via Sutton in Ashfield. MRB 709 an AEC Regent III with Brush H56R bodywork, new to Naylor's in 1950, was photographed in Westgate, Mansfield, sometime in the early fifties. When acquired by Trent in 1956, it took fleet number 1219 and remained in the operational fleet until 1959. After withdrawal, it was used by the Company for a time for practice in recovering overturned vehicles.

Operator taken over

During the post war period, to the end of 1968, only four independent operators were taken over, of which only one, Naylor's, owned a fleet of significant size, which passed into Trent ownership. The following selection of photographs illustrates vehicles of that company, before and after the take-over.

E Naylor & Sons of South Normanton

was taken over by Trent in July 1956. Several double deckers were operated, including this Guy Arab III with Northern Coachbuilders H56R bodywork, new in August 1948 and photographed in Ripley Market Place. It received fleetnumber 1217, and remained until 1959, following which it had a quite lengthy career with Reliance (R Store) of Stainforth near Doncaster.

Utility Guy Arab JNU 796 with Strachans UL55R bodywork was new to Naylor's in 1945, and was photographed at Mansfield on 14th July 1956, just a week after the takeover. It carries fleetnumber 1216, but this was changed to 1300 in September 1956, when it was realised that the body was to lowbridge configuration. It was repainted in Trent livery and the destination box modified to take a single line destination and three track route number blinds, remaining until 1959.

The ex Mansfield district AEC Regent, 1217, VO 8566, shown on page 24, is illustrated here after repainting into Trent livery.

This AEC Regal III, 643, NNU648, new in March 1949, carried a Burlingham C33F body. It remained in Trent service until 1959.

Two AEC Reliances, XRB 50/1, new in May 1955 joined Trent from Naylor's, taking the fleet numbers 646/7. As related in the text, they so impressed the Company that the next three batches of coaches were AEC Reliances, rather than the Leyland Tiger Cub, previously chosen. 646 was photographed operating a private hire from Derby, late in its time with the Company, the two being withdrawn in 1960, and sold, via Cowley, to contractors Wimpey.

Another AEC Regal III, 644, ORA 181, also with a Burlingham body, heads a line up of vehicles as drivers make their way to start a convoy for a day excursion. The location shown, opposite Derby's Central Bus Station, became swallowed up in the Cock Pitt Island and partly forms one side of the traffic circulatory area. the body on the vehicle, although fully fronted, shows clear derivation from that of 643, at the top right of the opposite page, in the styling rearwards from the cab.

Major Route Number Change - October 1953.

Prev No.	New No.	Terminal and Intermediate Points	Prev No.	New No.	Terminal and Intermediate Points
1	1	Derby-Alfreton, via Ripley	280	25A	Derby-Breadsall Crossing.
2	2	Derby-Belper, via Allestree and Duffield.	280	25B	Derby-Breadsall Church.
162	162	Derby-Matlock, via Duffield, Belper, Ambergate and Cromford.	27	25C	Derby-Ilkeston, via Breadsall Village, Morley and Smalley.
4	4	Derby-Buxton, via Belper, Ambergate, Cromford and Matlock.	29	26	Derby-Ilkeston, via Breadsall Village and Morley Moor.
5	5	Derby-Burton, via Repton.	30	30	Derby-Dovedale. (Summer only)
	5A	Derby-Havenbaulk Lane (Staker Lane)	31	31	Derby-Ashbourne, via Brailsford.
	5B	Derby-Mickleover via Havenbaulk Lane.	32	32	Derby-Ashbourne, via Cross o' th' Hands.
6	6	Derby-Burton, Direct	33	31B	Derby-Uttoxeter, via Ashbourne and Barrow hill.
7	7	Derby-Heanor, via Morely and Smalley.	34	34	Derby-Castle Donington, via Alvaston and Shardlow.
8	8	Derby-Nottingham, via Sandiacre.	36	36	Derby-Loughborough, via Castle Donington.
9	9	Derby-Spondon (White Swan), via Spondon Lane End.	37	37	Derby-Wirksworth.
10	9A	Derby-Spondon (Locko Road), via Spondon Lane End, Willow croft Road and White Swan.	38	38	Blackbrook-Derby.
			39	39	Shottle-Derby.
11	9B	Derby-Spondon (Huntley Avenue) via Spondon Lane End and White Swan.	40	20D	Derby-Ingleby
			41	40	Derby-Weston on Trent.
12	12	Derby-Borrowash-Derby (Circular)	42	33	Ashbourne-Leek, via Main Road.
13	13/13A	Derby-Borrowash-Derby (Circular)	43	33A	Ashbourne-Leek, via Cauldon Lowe.
14	9C	Derby-Spondon Village, via Sondon Lane End and Willow croft Rd.	44	14	Tenant Street-Roosevelt Avenue.(Derby Town Service).
15	15	Derby-Mickleover, via Western Road.	45	33B	Ashbourne-Leek, via Stanton, Cauldon Lowe and Waterhouses.
16		Derby-Mickleover LNER Station.	46	48	Derby, Cavendish, Blagreaves Lane. (Circular)
17	15A	Derby-Mickleover Pastures Hospital.	47	16	Hatton-Burton, via Tutbury and Rolleston.
18	18	Derby-Tutbury, via Hatton.	49	49	Derby, Cavendish, Blagreaves Lane. (Circular)
19	19	Derby-Melbourne.	50	50	Derby, Cavendish, Blagreaves Lane. (Circular)
19	19A	Derby-Melbourne, via Midland Station.	51	51	Derby, Cavendish, Blagreaves Lane. (Circular)
20	20	Derby-Chellaston and Swarkestone.	52	31A	Ashbourne-Mayfield.
21	21	Derby-Ashby.	53	31C	Rocester-Uttoxeter.
21	21A	Derby-Ashby, via Midland Station.	54	31D	Derby-Uttoxeter, via Ashbourne and Denstone.
22	22	Derby-Swadlincote, via Goseley Avenue and Brookdale Road.	55	55	Derby-Heanor.
22	22A	Derby-Swadlincote, via Midland Station.	158	55A	Derby-Heanor, via Horsley.
22	22B	Derby-Ticknall, via Midland Station, Kings Newton and Melbourne Station.	56	56	Derby-Allestree-Derby (Circular)
			57	57	Derby-Allestree-Derby (Circular)
22	23	Derby-Swadlincote, vai Brookdale Road and Goseley Avenue.	58	32A	Derby-Quarndon Church.
22	23A	Derby-Swadlincote, via Midland Station, Brookdale Road and Goseley Avenue.	59	32B	Derby-Park Nook.
			60	60	Nottingham-Hucknall, via Basford and Bulwell.
22	23B	Derby-Swadlincote, via Midland Station, Kings Newton, Brookdale Road and Goseley Avenue.	61	61	Nottingham-Mansfield, via Hucknall.
			61	61C	Nottingham-Sutton in Ashfield, via Hucknall.
			61	61D	Nottingham-Mansfield, via Hucknall and Newstead.
23	20C	Derby-Barrow and Twyford. Circular.	61	61E	Newstead-Nottingham.
24	24	Derby-Ilkeston, via Chaddesden, Stanley and West Hallam.	62	62	Nottingham-Mansfield, Direct via Harlow Wood.
25	25	Derby-Ilkeston, via Breadsall Windmill, Morley and Smalley.	63	63	Nottingham-Chesterfield.(Joint with East Midland 12A)
26	52	Derby-Barrow.			

Prev No.	New No.	Terminal and Intermediate Points	Prev No.	New No.	Terminal and Intermediate Points
64	64B	Nottingham-Doncaster.(Joint with East Midland 36)	99	99	Belper-Ripley, via Holbrook Moor.
65	65	Nottingham-Wilford Hill Cemetery	98	98	Belper-Heanor, via Horsley Woodhouse.
65A	65A	Nottingham-Clifton, via Wilford Hill Cemetery.	100	100	Alfreton-Mansfield, via South Normanton.
65B	65B	Nottingham-Loughborough, via Bunny and Ruddington.	104	104	Alfreton-Belper, via Somercotes, Leabrooks, and Ambergate.
66	66	Nottingham-Loughborough, via Hoton.	105	105	Belper-Ripley, via Pentrich
66	66A	Nottingham-Loughborough, via Ruddington Village.	106	106	Belper-Ripley, via Nether Heage
66	66B	Nottingham-Loughborough, via Wymeswold, Burton on the Wolds.	120	120	Loughborough-Markfield Sanatorium, via Nanpantan.
66	66C	Wymeswold-Loughborough.	121	121	Loughborough-Sileby.
68	73	Nottingham-East Bridgford. Joint with Skills.	122	122	Loughborough-Sileby (Jubilee Avenue).
69	69	Nottingham-Netherfield, via Colwick.	123	123	Loughborough-Nanpantan, via Forest Road.
70	70	Nottingham-Netherfield, via Gedling.	124	124	Loughborough-Willoughby, via Burton on the Wolds.
71	70A	Nottingham-Burton Joyce, via Netherfield, Gedling.	125	125	Loughborough-Nanpantan, via Beacon Road.
71	70C	Nottingham-Bulcote, via Conway Road.	126	126	Loughborough-Willoughby, via Hoton.
72	70B	Nottingham-Gunthorpe, via Burton Joyce.	127	127	Loughborough-Seagrave.
72	76A	Nottingham-Gunthorpe. (Direct).	128	128	Loughborough-Willoughby, via Walton and Burton on the Wolds.
73	73A	Nottingham-Shelford Village. Joint with Skills.	129	129	Loughboro' (Lemyngton Street)-Loughboro' (Empress Road)
74	74	Nottingham-Southwell, via Lowdham, Thurgaton, Halloughton.	131	131	Loughboro'(Tennyson Road)-Loughboro' (Broadway/Park Road).
74	74A	Nottingham-Southwell, via Caythorpe, Hoveringham, Fiskerton.	132	132	Loughboro' (Tennyson Road)-Loughboro' (Manor Rd/Broadway)
75	74B	Nottingham-Southwell, via Caythorpe, Hoveringham, Halloughton.	140	75	Hucknall-Gunthorpe (Summer only)
75	74C	Nottingham-Fiskerton.	141	75A	Bilborough-Gunthorpe (Summer only).
76	76	Nottingham-Burton Joyce.(Direct)	150	32C	Derby-Ashbourne, via Quarndon and Cross o' th' Hands.
77	79B	Nottingham-Radcliffe.	152	152	Derby-Church Broughton, via Sutton on the Hill.
78	79A	Nottingham-Bingham, via Radcliffe.	153	153	Derby-Hollington (Circular)
79	79	Nottingham-Grantham. Joint with Lincolnshire 33C.	154	154	Derby-Longford District (Circular)
81	81	East Bridgford-Newark, via Kneeton.	155	155	Derby-Mickleover Station (Circular)
82	82	East Bridgford-Bingham.	156	156	Derby-Mickleover Station (Circular)
83	61B	Nottingham-Kirkby in Ashfield (Hawthorne Crescent)	155/6	163	Derby-Radbourne Lane (Moorgate)
84	84	Nottingham-Sutton in Ashfield. (Direct).	157	157	Crich-Belper
87	67	Nottingham-Arnold.	158	158	Ambergate-Ripley (Nether Heage)
88	68	Nottingham-Stoke Bardolph, via Netherfield and Gedling..	159	159	Heanor-Kilburn Toll Bar, via Loscoe.
89	61A	Nottingham-Kirkby in Ashfield (Greenwood Drive)	160	160	Belper-Heanor, via Denby and Loscoe.
90	90	Derby-Belper, via Little Eaton and Holbrook.	161	161	Belper-Ripley, via Ambergate and Nether Heage
91	91	Belper-Ripley, via Kilburn Toll Bar and Marehay.	165	165	Ripley-Ilkeston.
92	91A	Belper-Ripley, via Kilburn Toll Bar and Street Lane.	197	197	Belper-Ripley, via Whatstandwell, Crich and Bull Bridge.
93	93	Belper-Ripley, via Kilburn Toll Bar and Openwoodgate.	280	25A	Derby-Breadsall Crossing.
94	94	Belper-Ripley, via Kilburn Toll Bar and Farlawn.	280	25B	Derby-Breadsall Church.
95	95	Belper-Ripley, via Ambergate.	625	625	Loughborough-Leicester, via Mountsorrell.
96	96	Crich-Ripley.	626	626	Loughborough-Leicester, via Birstall.
97	97	Whatstandwell-Ripley.	629	629	Loughborough-Leicester, via Sileby.

Note: This list does not follow on exactly from that on page 163 of Part One. During the period from the previous major route number change, in December 1934, 1934, some services were individually altered. This was for operational reasons such as a need to use the number for another service, or a route may have changed terminus but retained the same number, or a service may have been withdrawn, and its number re-used for another service.

Services Listed in Timetable Book for 1965. (Two to three years before the end of the BET era.)

Route No	Service Details	Route No	Service Details
1	Derby-Alfreton, via Little Eaton, Denby Swanwick and Leabrooks.	32-32C	Derby-Ashbourne, via Quarndon.
2	Derby-Belper, via Allestree, Duffield and Milford.	33, 33A/B	Ashbourne-Leek, via Waterhouses.
4, 4B	Derby-Buxton, via Matlock. Joint with North Western.	34, 34A/B	Derby-Castle Donington, via Alvaston and Shardlow.
5	Derby-Burton, via Littleover, Findern and Repton.	36, 36A	Derby-Loughborough, via Shardlow.
5A, 5B	Derby-Mickleover, via Havenbaulk Lane.	37	Derby-Wirksworth, via Allestree, Duffield and Idridgehay.
5H	Derby-Bretby (orthapaedic Hospital)	38	Derby-Blackbrook, via Duffield and Farnah Green. (Friday only).
6	Derby-Burton, DIRECT, via Clay Mills.	39	Derby-Shottle via Turnditch and Windley. (Friday only).
7	Derby-Heanor, via Breadsall (Windmill), Broomfield, and Smalley.	40	Derby-Weston on Trent.
8	Derby- Nottingham, via Borrowash, Sandiacre and Stapleford.	44	Derby-Chesterfield, via Alfreton. Joint with East Midland and Midland General.
8H	Derby-Draycott Hospital.		
9, 9A/B/C	Derby-Spondon Village via Spondon Lane.	48-51A	Derby-Blagreaves Lane. (Circular). Joint with Derby Corporation.
10	Derby-Kirk Hallam.	52	Derby-Barrow on Trent, via Stenson.
12, 12A, 13	Derby-Borrowash, via Ockbrook.	55, 55A	Derby-Heanor, via Kilburn Toll Bar and Horsley Woodhouse.
		56, 56A	Derby-Allestree (Circular), via Kedleston Road.
14	Derby-Chaddesden (Roosevelt Avenue) Joint with Derby Corporation.	57, 57A	Derby-Allestree (Circular), via Duffield Road, Darley Abbey and Kedleston Road.
15, 15A/B	Derby-Mickleover, via Western Road.		
15A	Derby-Mickleover, BR Station.	58, 58A	Derby-Quarndon (Church).
15B	Derby-Mickleover, Mental Hospital.	60, 60A/C	Nottingham-Hucknall (Ruffs Estate).
16	Hatton-Burton on Trent, via Rolleston.	60B	Nottingham-Hucknall (Beauvale Estate).
17	Burton on Trent-Rolleston, via Horninglow.	60D	Nottingham-Linby.
18	Derby-Tutbury, via Chain Lane, Mickleover, Etwall, and Hatton.	61, 61C/D/H	Nottingham-Mansfield, via Hucknall.
18H	Derby-Etwall Hospital.		
19-23B	Derby-Sawdlincote, via Allenton, Chellaston, and Melbourne.	61A/B	Nottingham-Kirkby in Ashfield.
20, 20B	Derby-Chellaston.	62	Nottingham-Mansfield, via Redhill and Harlow Wood.
20C	Derby-Twyford, via Barrow.	62H	Nottingham-Newstead Hospital.
20D	Derby-Ingleby, via Swarkestone.	63	Nottingham-Chesterfield, via Mansfield. Joint with East Midland.
21, 21A	Derby-Ashby, via Allenton, Chellaston, Melbourne, Wilson and Lount.	64	Nottingham-Doncaster, via Worksop. Joint with East Midland.
24	Derby-Ilkeston, via Chaddesden, Stanley and West Hallam.	65, 65A	Nottingham-Clifton, via Wilford Hill.
25	Derby-Ilkeston, via Breadsall (Windmill), Morley and W. Hallam.	65B-66C	Nottingham-Loughborough, via Ruddington.
25A	Derby-Breadsall Village.	67, 67B/C	Nottingham-Hucknall, via Gedling.
25C	Derby-Ilkeston, via Breadsall Village, Morley and W. Hallam.	67A, 69, 69A, 70	Nottingham-Gedling, via Netherfield.
26	Derby-Ilkeston, via Smalley Mill.		
27	Derby-Breadsall (Scarborough Rise). Joint with Derby Corporation.	68	Nottingham-Stoke Bardolph.
27H	Derby-Derwent Hospital.	70A, 70B	Nottingham-Gunthorpe, via Burton Joyce.
28	Derby-Derby, via Hollington.(Circular)	70C	Nottingham-Bulcote.
29	Derby-Derby, via Longford. (Circular)	73	Nottingham-East Bridgford, via Radcliffe.
30	Derby-Mackworth Estate.	73A	Nottingham-Shelford Village.
30D	Derby-Dovedale. (Summer only)	74, 74A/B/C	Nottingham-Southwell, via , Lowdham.
31-31E	Derby-Uttoxeter, via Ashbourne.		

Route No	Service Details	Route No	Service Details
75	Bilborough-Gunthorpe, via Gedling.	100	Alfreton-Mansfield, via South Normanton.
76	Nottingham-Burton Joyce, via Carlton.	102	Ripley-Ripley (Ash Crescent).
76A	Nottingham-Gunthorpe, via Carlton.	103	Ripley-Ilkeston, via Horsley Woodhouse
77	Nottingham-Gedling, via Carlton.	104	Alfreton-Belper, via Somercotes, Leabrooks and Ambergate.
79	Nottingham-Grantham, via Bottesford. Joint with Lincolnshire 33C.	105	Belper-Ripley, via Pentrich
79A/8	Nottingham-Bingham, via radcliffe.	106	Belper-Ripley, via Nether Heage
80	Nottingham-Retford, via Ollerton. Joint with East Midland 37.	107	Ambergate-Ripley, via Nether Heage
81	East Brdgford-Newark.	108	Belper-Ripley, via Ambergate-Nether Heage
82	East Bridgford-Granby, via Newark.	120	Loughborough-Markfield Sanatorium
84, 84B	Nottingham-Sutton in Ashfield, via Hucknall.	121/2/7	Loughborough-Seagrave, via Sileby
88	Netherfield-Bramcote.	123/5	Loughborough (Sharpley Road)-Nanpantan
90	Derby-Belper, via Little Eaton and Holbrook.	124	Loughborough-Willoughby, via Wymeswold.
91	Belper-Ripley, via Kilburn Toll Bar.	126	Loughborough-Willoughby, via Hoton.
92	Belper-Shottle, via Blackbrook.	128	Loughborough-Willoughby, via Walton.
93	Belper-Ripley, via Openwoodgate.	130	Loughboro' (Sharpley Road)-Loughboro' (Empress Road)
94	Belper-Ripley, via Farlawn.	131	Loughboro' (Rupert Brooke Road)-Loughboro' (Hambledon Cres.)
95	Belper-Ripley, via Ambergate.	132	Loughboro' (Rupert Brooke Road)-Loughboro' (Manor Rd/Br'dw'y)
96,96A/B	Belper-Ripley, via Whatstandwell and Crich.	133, 135	Loughborough (Midland Station)-Nanpantan
97	Belper-Crich, via Bull Bridge.	134	Loughboro' (Hambledon Crescent)-Bishops Meadow (Industrial Est.)
98, 98A/B	Belper-Heanor, via Kilburn Toll Bar.	625, 626	Derby-Leicester, via Loughborough
99	Belper-Ripley, via Holbrook Moor.	655, 659	Loughborough-Leicester, via Sileby

Express Services

X1	Derby-Manchester.	X18	Loughborough-Blackpool
X2	Nottingham-Manchester.	X19	Derby, Nottingham-Clacton-on-Sea
X3	Derby, Nottingham-Skegness	X20	Derby, Nottingham-Hunstanton and Cromer
X4	Derby, Nottingham-Mablethorpe and Sutton-on-Sea	X21	Derby, Nottingham-Hunstanton
X5	Derby, Nottingham-Cleethorpes	X22	Nottingham, Derby-Pwllheli
X6	Nottingham, Derby-Blackpool	X23, X24	Manchester-Skegness
X7	Derby, Nottingham-Great Yarmouth	X25	Loughborough-Llandudno
X8	Belper, Ripley, Alfreton, Mansfield-Skegness	X26	Alfreton, Ripley, Belper, Derby-Rhyl, Abergele, Colwyn Bay, Llandudno
X9	Alfreton, Ripley, Belper-Blackpool	X27	Derby, Nottingham-Cambridge
X10	Derby, Mansfield-Bridlington and Scarborough	X28	Derby, Nottingham-Felixstowe
X11	Hucknall-Skegness	X29	Derby, Nottingham-Southend
X13	Alfreton-Great Yarmouth. Joint with Midland General.	X31	Barrow-on-Soar-Skegness
X14	Mansfield-Great Yarmouth	X34	Derby-East Midlands Airport
X15	Derby, Nottingham-Lowestoft	X42	Nottingham-Derby (Joint with Barton)
X16	Hucknall-Cleethorpes	MX4	Alfreton-London, via Derby and Loughborough (Joint with Midland General, United Counties and Yellow ay)
X17	Loughborough-Great Yarmouth		

Acquired Operators and Services, 1945 - 68.

Takeover Date	Operator Name	Routes	Allocated Route No.	Vehicles Acquired	Amount Paid	Add'l Note
23rd January 1946	J Riley, Belper.	Belper(King St)-Derby(Baseball Ground) (Express) Excursions and Tours from Belper Market Place and from Heage (Black Boy Inn).		None	£700	
18th September 1953 (wef 20th Sept 1953)	Allen's Motor Services, Mountsorrel.	Loughborough(Lemington Street)-Nanpantan. Loughborough(Lemington Street)-Loughborough (Shelthorpe). Loughborough(Lemington Street)-Loughborough (Outwoods Drive) Loughborough(Empress Works)-Thorpe Acre Village. Loughborough(Brush Works)-L'ghbor'gh (Shelthorpe) Loughborough-Leicester, via Woodhouse Loughborough-Leicester, via Mountsorrel Loughborough-Leicester City Football Ground. Loughborough-Skegness, via Leicester (Express) Mountsorrel-Sileby Excursions and Tours from Mountsorrel, Syston. and Loughborough.	123/5	None	£12 500	1
21st July 1955 (wef 31st July 1955)	H S North Transport, Derby.	Belper(Strutt St)-Shottle Cross Roads	92	None	£2 500	2
Late 1955/early 1956	Birmingham & Midland Motor Omnibus Co, Ltd.	Leicester-Loughborough (part share) Loughborough-Derby	625/55/9 36	None	£6 660 £3 838 plus £368	3
7th July 1956	E Naylor & Sons, Ltd, South Normanton.	Alfreton-Mansfield, via South Normanton South Normanton-Derby(Baseball Ground)(Express) Excursions & Tours from South Normanton	100	9	£37 500	
1st February 1959	Birmingham & Midland Motor Omnibus Co, Ltd.	Leicester-Loughborough (20% of service acquired from W Boyer, Rothley)	625/55/9	None	£2 700	

Note	Remark
1	**Allen's Motor Services, Mountsorrel.** The Loughborough-Nanpantan and Loughborough-Brush Works services were jointly operated with Trent. Mr and Mrs Allen were also Directors of Kemp & Shaw, Ltd, which was taken over by Midland Red.
2	**HS North Transport, Derby.** HS North sold an earlier business to Trent in 1935. This service had been acquired by North, from P& J W Poundall in 1936. Trent extended the service to Cross o' the Hands.
3	**Birmingham & Midland Motor Omnibus Co, Ltd.** The payments shown were made to the Birmingham & Midland Motor Omnibus Co, Ltd (Midland Red) following their purchase on 30th July 1955 of the businesses of Kemp & Shaw Ltd and Allen's' Motor Services, which ran the services shown. It was agreed that Trent would participate in the additional service between Leicester and Loughborough, on a mileage basis, for which Trent paid BMMO £6660. Trent also acquired the entire Loughborough-Derby service, for which the Minute Book states it paid BMMO £3838, although the BMMO Minute Book indicates a figure of £2 431. The additional £368 was paid by Trent to BMMO at the time of the latter's take-over of W Boyer, of Rothley, following a re-division of the goodwill payment for the Kemp & Shaw and Allen's Services between Leicester and Loughborough.

Liveries of the BET era

The early Commercial Car Hirers vehicles were, according to the Derbyshire Motor Tax Records, painted green with white lines, or dark green, and this applied to CH 405 and CH 537 respectively. Later vehicles, beginning with CH 637, were painted a colour described as "French Grey" , a popular colour for charabancs at the time, and this colour was continued by Trent until the first Tilling Stevens Petrol Electrics arrived in 1915. The first eleven of these were painted green, the shade unspecified. In 1916, two Tilling Stevens, CH 1373 and CH 1419, were delivered once again grey, the latter in a colour described as "light grey", and the former in "blue grey". The next two vehicles, delivered in 1917, were in dark green, but the following vehicles, which arrived in 1919, were green and cream. This is thought to have continued until 1923, and in some cases, there was a reference to the colour as light green. The exact shade of green will, almost certainly, never be known. However, Mr Neville Evans, of Plumtree, near Nottingham, who lived in Uttoxeter New

Road from the early 1920s until 1972, states that the colour was not unlike the apple shade formerly used by the erstwhile Southdown Motor Services. This would not be inconsistent with the Motor Tax reference to "light green".

In 1924, the Tilling Stevens TS6s arrived, and these were the first vehicles to be painted in the new livery of red, said at the time to match the livery of neighbouring Midland Red, with which Trent had just begun joint operations on a service between Loughborough and Leicester. Readers of Part One will recall that it was at this time that Mr O C Power, Traffic Manager of Midland Red, became a member of the Trent Board. The shade used was generally referred to as "BET Light Red", and it continued to be used as the main fleet colour until 1972, when a new shade of red was adopted. Where applicable, the Light Red was topped with a white roof, although this probably had an off white appearance, due to the use of varnish to protect the finish.

Application of BET Light Red varied down the years, and it was sometimes

This painting, which was commissioned in 1963, on the occasion of the Company's Golden Jubilee, provides an idea of how the vehicles might have looked in the early green livery. It shows a Tilling Stevens TS3 Petrol Electric, crossing Whatstandwell Bridge in 1920 - a location that does not look greatly different, even today.

A rare pre-war colour photograph of one of the 1937 Weymann bodied AEC Regents at Huntingdon Street Bus Station, Nottingham. The picture is a little out of focus and, inevitably, the colour print has deteriorated with the passage of time, but it is included to give an impression of the fleet in the pre-war years.

combined with a maroon shade, known as "BET Dark Red". The Tilling Stevens TS6s appear to have been all Light Red, with lining which may have been gold in colour, or straw. The fleetname was in gold colouring, the style being as reproduced on the cover of Part One, placed centrally on the lower panels, and sometimes on the front and back, in a smaller size.

With the arrival of a batch of SOS QLs in 1928, a brown waistband moulding was added to the livery, and this continued until 1935, when a streamlined livery was introduced, this being fashionable, at the time. A streamline polished moulding swept down from the waistrail, beginning at a point above the rear wheel arch, and sweeping down to the lower edge of the panels at the rear corner and continuing along the lower edge of the rear panels. The area between the brown waistband and the polished moulding was painted Dark Red and there was often a fleetname placed centrally on the rear Dark Red panels.

In some cases, on coaches and vehicles that would nowadays be termed dual purpose, the gold fleetname on the sides was replaced by a raised diamond in polished aluminium, enclosing the initials "TMT", also in raised aluminium. The livery style continued until the last SOS SONs were delivered in the early years of the war. After the war, the streamlining was discontinued and, indeed, removed from many vehicles. However, twenty AEC Regal IIIs delivered in 1950 featured twin streamline mouldings, enclosing Dark Red, although the Dark Red was replaced by Light Red early in the life of the vehicles.

Double deckers re-entered the fleet in 1936, after a break, and these were overall Light Red, with a white roof and with Dark Red bands on both waistrails and the lower deck cant rail.

When war came, there were some significant changes. All white roofs were painted grey, to make them less conspicuous from aircraft, although the white was reinstated towards the end of the war. The last Daimler COG5s, delivered in 1940 with Weymann bodies to generally peacetime standards, were delivered in a matt grey finish. In 1942, a number of single deck and coach chassis were rebodied with double deck bodies by Willowbrook, and these were received from the factory in battleship grey, with dark grey bands replacing the Dark Red waistrail and cant rail bands. Subsequent deliveries were in plain grey with no varnish, but from October 1944, the livery became overall Light Red, with a white roof and, later, lining in a straw colour, but no Dark Red bands.

 Starting in March 1947, a new livery was introduced of Light Red, with white (or ivory) roof and window surrounds, straw lining and Dark Red wings. This may have been influenced by the new General Manager, Mr James Forster, who had joined the Company from Northern General. The latter company used a similar style, at the time, although using BET Dark Red as the main colour, rather than the Light Red used by Trent. Some newer SOSs and AEC Regals retained a dark red waistband with aluminium mouldings.

Coaches were Dark Red with white trim, or ivory with Dark Red trim, which gradually replaced the previous style and, in time, Light Red trim replaced the Dark Red trim. During the thirties, the Company had used a garter fleetname on some vehicles featuring a circular garter incorporating the full company name, and enclosing the initials "TMT Co". This continued to be used for a

The garter device, used in the thirties, and continued on some vehicles after the war.

time on some of the older coaches, until they were withdrawn in the fifties.

The standard post war fleetname continued to be in a large gold coloured style, but was gradually reduced in size over a period of time, becoming yellow with black edging, sometime in the mid fifties. With the arrival of the first Leylands, in 1951, the straw lining was abandoned, and was gradually removed from existing vehicles, as they were repainted. From 1959, a new style of fleetname was introduced, in a smaller size using sans serif black edge lettering, as reproduced on the cover of this volume, and many operators were introducing more modern styles of lettering during this period. This was usually placed centrally on double deckers and single deck buses, but on dual purposes vehicles and coaches was usually placed in a more forward position and indeed as the length of single deck buses increased, the fleetname was placed in a more forward position on these also. From 1961, the fleetname on rear engine buses was placed in the "temple" position above the cab and the entrance.

In the 1950s, many dual purpose vehicles, combining some of the attributes of a bus and a coach joined the fleet. These were painted in bus livery, but with additional areas of ivory, to distinguish their status. From 1961, dual purpose vehicles were, like coaches, painted predominantly ivory, but with varying amounts of red relief, depending on the body style and polished moulding arrangement. Some dual purpose vehicles delivered in 1955 had a small fleetname enclosed in polished mouldings, and some had a polished metal fleetname, similarly enclosed. Many coaches had a raised metal fleetname, whilst the 1959 dual purpose Tiger Cubs had the fleetname in an italicised form of gold lettering, in a style used by several BET Companies at the time. However, with the advent of the new sans serif fleetname, all of the variations were gradually removed at repaint. This style of lettering, and the liveries described continued beyond the period covered by this volume, until 1972.

611, ACH 441, shown in preservation to illustrate the use of Dark Red in the coach livery. When new, the vehicle would also have been Dark Red above the polished waistrail moulding. This was an intermediate livery, as later the Dark Red trim was repainted Light Red. The Gothic style fleetname, used on some coaches after the war was replaced on these vehicles by a raised, polished aluminium style placed centrally below the polished waistrail.

The 1955 dual purpose Tiger Cubs introduced a livery based on the bus style with additional cream to distinguish them from standard buses. 140, HRC 140, at Manchester, shows its allocation to Alfreton depot by the yellow background to the number plate. The vehicle had lost most of the bright metal originally fitted on the front panel.

1145, ACH 635, an AEC Regent of 1948, shows a variation of the new livery adopted from 1947. However, when new, the canopy and the cab and front bulkhead window surrounds would have been ivory, and there would have been straw lining on the lower panels, with a larger gold coloured fleetname.

749, JCH 259, one of the first PD2s with lightweight Orion bodies by Metro Cammell, looks fresh from the paint shop without any external advertising at Loughborough.

115

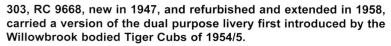

303, RC 9668, new in 1947, and refurbished and extended in 1958, carried a version of the dual purpose livery first introduced by the Willowbrook bodied Tiger Cubs of 1954/5.

163, VCH 163, new at the same time as 391, has an almost identical body structure, save for the extended skirt panels between the wheel arches. However, as it had a dual purpose internal configuration, with improved seats, the external livery had a greater area of ivory, to good effect. At the back, there was a shaped panel of red around, and including, the boot.

The style of bodywork carried by 391, VCH 841, new in 1961 originally numbered 841, could be seen all over the land in BET, municipal and independent fleets. 391 carries the standard Trent bus livery used at the end of, and beyond, the BET era.

Northern Counties' well proportioned body style for rear engine chassis, which was considered amongst the best in the sixties, and was greatly enhanced by the simple style of Trent livery. 621, 621 CCH awaits a turn of duty to Allestree on the 57 service, via Duffield Road and Darley Abbey

1962 vintage 221, 221 CCH, was one of the first batch of 36ft (10.97m) vehicles in the fleet and introduced an attractive new livery style for dual purpose vehicles. the general layout of the polished mouldings was to Willowbrook's standard, but the frontal style was specific to Trent, and added considerably to the appearance

251, ECH 251C, of 1965 and also bodied by Willowbrook, was originally painted in the same style as 221 on the left. However, after spray painting was introduced, the livery was found to be complicated for masking up. Initially, the ivory skirt was eliminated, but later the livery changed to this style, copied from the Alexander Y type bodywork, as shown on the cover.

The livery for coaches was invariably adapted to suit the polished mouldings fitted by the coachbuilder, but normally involved a greater area of ivory. Coach 2, 122 FCH, a Leyland Leopard of 1963, features the stylish Plaxton Panorama coachwork, a trend setter which is now almost a classic of its era.

503, MRC 503E, a Daimler Fleetline, was amongst the last vehicles delivered whilst the Company was still in BET ownership and shows the final style of livery in the BET era. Note the fleetname, in the temple position. The livery style, although simple, was considered to be one of the more attractive amongst the territorial companies, at a time when many were adopting single colour liveries with only minimal relief.

Tickets of the BET era

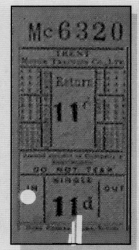

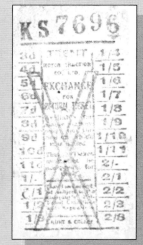

Selection of pre-war Bell Punch tickets

Selection of Setright Insert tickets

Ultimate tickets, used on services
operated jointly with
Derby Corporation

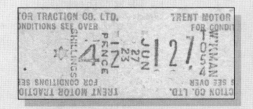
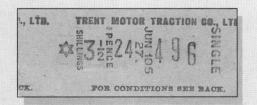

Selection of Setright Speed tickets

Publicity in the BET era

A small selection of publicity booklets issued by the Company over the years to 1940. The first three, from top left, are booklets describing places of interest which could be visited using the Company's bus services. The first from 1922, and the second from 1924, whilst the remainder are as dated on the cover. The other four are brochures for the Company's coach holidays. All are reproduced at 40% of their original size.

Timetable Covers

Some of the timetable booklets issued by the Company, are shown here, from the first, in November 1917, until the mid sixties. The first book was cream in colour, whilst in the early twenties, the books were green. From about mid 1924, the covers were tan or beige, with red and blue or black printing. After the war, the covers were off white, with red and black printing, and then a style with white printing on a maroon background was adopted in the fifties. The special cover for the Diamond Jubilee edition in 1963 was followed by a return to the previous style. However, from 1965, a new format, approximately A5 in size, was adopted by the industry collectively, and those produced by Trent in this style are shown on the lower right. These also incorporated a new style of map which showed other operators' services, as well as those of Trent.

1

2

3

4

5

6

7

Key

1.	November 1917, Issue No 1	7.	June 1949
2.	June 1921	8.	May 1956
3.	May 1924	9.	Golden Jubilee Edition, April 1963
4.	September 1924	10.	May 1964
5.	December 1936	11.	June 1965
6.	December 1939	12.	May 1966

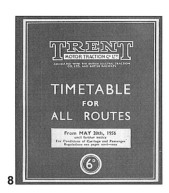

8

9

10

11

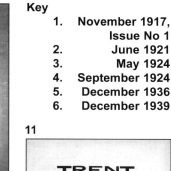

12

Depots and Other Premises

ALFRETON DEPOT

Alfreton is an old market town, but was also for many years a centre of the coal mining industry, the Nottinghamshire and Derbyshire coal field being particularly productive. The mining industry has now gone, however, and a diverse range of replacement industries has sprung up, much of it on land reclaimed from mining.

Commercial Car Hirers opened the first Alfreton Depot in Hall Street in 1912, and a photograph is shown on page 6 of Part One. As Trent was formed in October 1913, and took over the Commercial Car Hirer's business, Alfreton can lay claim to being the birthplace of the company. The first Trent Depot was opened in 1920, in Limes Avenue, but this was converted to offices in 1926 when a new depot was opened on land acquired from Mr W J Whysall, in Gooker Lane, at its junction with Derby Road, Watchorn. Following the formation of the National Bus Company, in 1969, which brought Trent and Midland General under common ownership, to be described in the next volume, Midland General's depot in King Street was modernised and extended, which was completed in January 1976. An earlier arrangement, in 1962, when the two companies were in different, separate ownership, had seen two Trent vehicles parked overnight at Midland General's Alfreton depot.

The former Trent depot was poorly sited for modern traffic conditions in relation to the adjacent road junction, and planning permission for expansion and reconstruction could not be obtained, so the opportunity to join forces with Midland General was particularly beneficial. The new depot was first shared by both companies, and then taken over by Trent when it became responsible for the management of Midland General in 1972, and fully absorbed that Company in 1976, again to be described in the next volume. The original depot still stands at the time of writing, although a wall has been constructed to in fill the original door opening, and the premises are now used for industrial purposes. To begin with, it had a forecourt, but this was built over in 1926. A further extension followed in 1935, and this took in a site alongside.

In earlier days, the depot was responsible for vehicles operating services from Alfreton to Mansfield, Ripley, Belper and Derby, and later the depot also supplied the Trent allocation for the Derby-Chesterfield service which was operated jointly by Trent, East Midland and Midland General from 1954. During 1965, Trent started a service between Alfreton and London, via Derby, Loughborough and the M1 motorway, which was operated jointly with Yelloway, United Counties and Midland General, each company operating the one journey each way per day for a three months at a time in rotation. Alfreton depot supplied the Trent vehicle for this service, which was considered a prestigious working, allocated only to the most experienced drivers.

Alfreton depot in Gooker Lane, Watchorn. The picture must have been taken soon after the depot opened, for it shows the original forecourt and an SOS S type, a Tilling Stevens TS3 inside the building and, probably, a Thornycroft J double decker in the corner behind the wall. The appearance of the building is similar to that of an early aircraft hangar.

This photograph was probably taken in the thirties, for an SOS IM6, 125 of 1931 is visible, with an SOS ODD type on the left and Morris 15cwt van no 33, RC 29, also of 1931, on the right. The building has now been extended over the forecourt.

An early fifties cross section of the fleet is revealed by this photograph, which also shows the additional extension, on the left, added in 1935. Visible, from left to right are, 403, a 1939 SOS SON, 101, a 1950 AEC Regal III, 1063, a 1939 Daimler COG5 rebodied in 1948 and 721, a 1946 AEC Regal ii, all with Willowbrook bodies and part of the depot allocation at the time. Also the depot's van, 4, CCH 966, a 1951 Commer, derived from the contemporary Hillman Minx saloon car.

ASHBOURNE DEPOT

Ashbourne is a small market town, very much seen as the gateway to the Peak District. It will be recalled that the first Commercial Car Hirers service, started in 1909, ran between Derby and Ashbourne. Locally, its main claim to fame is the annual Shrovetide Football Match when local people turn out to get the ball to either Sturston Mill or Clifton Mill, which are at each end of the Town and are the "goals".

In the early days, Commercial Car Hirers stored their vehicles overnight in the yard of the Green Man and Black's Head Royal Hotel. Later, there was an arrangement with Mr J Harrison for washing and storage of vehicles and a booking agency, following the take-over of his business in 1917.

The original Trent garage was leased from A R Atkey & Co, Ltd, the Nottingham based motor dealers, and occupied from August 1933. In 1953, a new access was formed from Compton Street to spare ground in front of the building to provide parking for two double deckers.

The present garage was opened on the same site, on 1st July 1958, but at the time of writing the Company occupies only half, the other half being let out to a garden supplies company. However, in earlier times, when the Company ran coach holidays, it was used for the storage of de-licenced coaches during the winter months.

The Company took over Bayliss of Ashbourne, running to Derby, in 1930, S P Radford of Mayfield in 1932, running to Leek, and A Slater of Mayfield, in 1934, running to Uttoxeter. At the time of writing, only services to Derby and Mayfield are operated, apart from a peak hour journey on the Mayfield service extended to Uttoxeter.

A view of Ashbourne depot, taken when newly opened in 1958.

BELPER DEPOT

A small town, on the side of the Derwent Valley, Belper is one of the oldest industrial towns in the Midlands. It was the site of an early mill set up by the partnership of Richard Arkwright and Jedidiah Strutt over 200 years ago, following Arkwright's pioneering mill (the first in the world), opened in 1771 at nearby Cromford. Nowadays there is a range of industry in the town and it is also a dormitory town for employment in Derby, Nottingham and elsewhere.

The former Chapman depot in Campbell Street, Belper, probably taken in the early thirties, fairly soon after the takeover. The building was completely demolished in the subsequent improvements.

Trent first reached Belper on 1st May 1914, when a daily service was started between Derby and Ambergate, with two journeys extended to Matlock on Sundays. In August, a further service was added on top of this, with journeys running between Derby and Belper only. In those early days buses were stored overnight in the yard of the town's Lion Hotel.

In May 1929, the business of George Chapman & Sons was taken over and this included garage premises on part of the site of the present depot. Other businesses in the area were also taken over, including P & J W Poundall, and E Barlow, both of Belper, and others running into the Town, giving a network, based on the town, which served Derby, Ripley, Heanor and Crich. There were also, in earlier times when people placed greater reliance on public transport for the journey to work, a wide range of works services operated from the Depot.

The former Chapman premises were too small to meet the Company's needs in the Town, and dormy sheds were used in Wellington Court, New Road and Strutt Street. There were frequent complaints about congestion, noise and fumes (even in the thirties!). As a result of these, the Council threatened at one point to consider fixing bus stopping points in Market Place, at the top of King Street, which would have involved the Company in inconvenience in operation and much dead mileage, if there was not the prospect of early change. Although it had the intention of making changes, the Company had to put off these complaints, but eventually additional land was acquired on an adjoining site in Chapel Street. The former Chapman premises were demolished, leading to the provision of a much larger and unusual building serving the function of bus station by day and depot by night.

The enlarged plot of land extended from Chapel Street, part of the main A6 Derby road to Campbell Street which runs parallel to it, with a significant level difference of some 1.8metres (6ft) rising from Chapel Street to Campbell Street. Work on the new building started in 1939, but had to be curtailed in 1940, owing to a wartime shortage of building materials with only the Chapel Street part completed.

The remaining part of the building was finally completed and opened in 1952. The level difference

The unusual depot at Belper, serving as a bus station during the day and a garage overnight. A Weymann bodied Tiger Cub noses out of the doorway in this late fifties picture.

referred to earlier led to the need for a vehicle ramp from Campbell Street into the vehicle area, and this ramp features a slight dogleg in its alignment. With the shorter vehicles in use in 1950, this presented no problem. However, the increasing length of vehicles has led a number of unwary drivers to leave deposits of red paint on the inside corner of the adjacent wall, as they drive down the ramp to the vehicle area! Passengers use a separate passage to gain access to the bus station from Campbell Street. Additional land was acquired in 1956, and a parking area constructed on it the following year.

CASTLE DONINGTON DEPOT

In the late 1920s, E & H Frakes built their garage in Ernest Frakes' garden in Station Road, Castle Donington. It was a wood and corrugated iron structure which accommodated two Chevrolet and later two Bedford buses. The Frakes business was acquired by Barton in 1946, and the garage was sold on to Trent with the Castle Donington-Derby service. Trent used it to accommodate one single decker, and there was parking for another full size vehicle in front of the building. The depot was later sold.

DERBY (MEADOW ROAD) DEPOT

Since 1967, the sole operating depot in Derby, the original Meadow Road Depot was opened in 1937 on land acquired from the LMS Railway. During the war, an extension was built at the back to house and service gas producer units which, in common with other major companies, the Company was obliged to operate. This was completed in 1943 but, in the event, the trailers were not used for very long. However, it was not until 1951 that an alternative use was found and the extension was converted into a paint shop, to handle the majority of the painting, which had previously been carried out at Central Works in Uttoxeter New Road.

Additional land, known as the Peel Foundry site, to the south of the depot was acquired in February, 1956, with the intention of extending the depot, which was much better placed in relation to Derby bus station than the depot at Uttoxeter New Road, and this held the prospect of eliminating much dead mileage. It took some years before this plan came to fruition, a start being made in 1965 when the foundry site was cleared and two new running sheds with service lane between were constructed, being brought into use in March, 1966. The original depot was then converted into a dock shop for the whole of the Derby based fleet, this being brought into use in October, 1966.

The new facilities enabled the entire Derby operational fleet to be housed in the depot, and all major repairs for vehicles allocated to the depot and to the depots at Alfreton, Belper, Melbourne and Shipley to be carried out there. The vehicles based at Shipley and Melbourne could also receive daily servicing at Meadow Road, allowing those two depots to be reduced to the status of dormy sheds.

In 1976, a disastrous fire occurred in the centre (B) running shed in the early hours of one morning and this resulted in the loss of twenty-seven buses and damage to a number of others. The running shed was severely damaged and had to be reconstructed, being returned to service in April 1978. The full story of this event is told in a subsequent volume, but it is of great significance, that despite the scale of the disaster and its early morning time of occurrence, not a single mile of service was lost the following morning.

The depot provides vehicles for all the Derby based services, a task that it previously shared with Uttoxeter New Road, when that was an operational depot.

Meadow Road depot, photographed in 1966, on completion of the expansion and improvement works. A garage, with closed doors on the left of the picture, was the original depot, and this was converted into a dock shop. B garage, in the centre of the picture was severely damaged by fire in 1976, but was subsequently reconstructed in more or less its original form. C garage, on the right, is now largely used, at the time of writing, by Derby Community Transport.

DERBY (UTTOXETER NEW ROAD) DEPOT & CENTRAL WORKS

Derby originated as a market and industrial town, and was created a city by the Queen as part of her Silver Jubilee celebrations in 1977. It has claim to the very first factory in the world, the Silk Mill in Full Street, and there remain some notable industries. These include, amongst others, Rolls- Royce (aero engines only, the cars are built elsewhere), Royal Crown Derby China, Qualcast Mowers, Courtaulds (formerly British Celanese) and, of course, the railway, although the present Adtranz manufacturing facility is but a shadow of the massive works originally created by the Midland Railway. Although the Company started at Alfreton, very few years passed before it moved to Derby, where the Head Office and major facilities remained until the move to Heanor was completed in 1997.

The first depot in Derby was on London Road, close to The Spot, and the building still stands today,

The second Derby depot, opened in 1915, fitted into the apex of Uttoxeter New Road (shown here) and Great Northern Road. This view shows the building after it had been converted to a Central Works, for which the main entrance was in Great Northern Road, and extended. When new, the entrance was off Uttoxeter New Road, directly beneath the raised Trent facia. The two extensions to the building can be identified, two bays at the far end, being the 1935 extension, whilst the four bays at the nearest end are the 1938 extension. The two houses on the right of the picture were used as offices by the engineering department.

as illustrated on page 14 of Part One. They were occupied from early 1914, until new premises were opened on the western side of Uttoxeter New Road, at the junction with Great Northern Road in mid 1915.

The new premises were extended in 1919 and in 1920-22, but in 1924 were superseded as a running depot in 1924, when a new depot was constructed on the opposite side of the road. The previous depot was then converted for use as a Central Works. In 1934, two houses adjacent to the western end of the building were purchased and demolished, and an extension constructed to house a stores and paint shop was completed in 1935. In 1936, further houses were purchased adjacent to the eastern of the building, and these two were demolished, with an extension being constructed to provide accommodation for bodybuilding and a new machine shop on the first floor, completed in 1938. Before long, further houses were purchased adjacent to the eastern end, and converted into offices for the engineering department.

The Works housed a very wide range of functions, and included chassis dock, body shop, paint shop, machine and unit shop, fuel pump and injection shop, trimming shop, electricians shop, battery charging shop, blacksmiths shop and an extensive stores. However, the paint shop was transferred to Derby Meadow Road depot in 1951. In 1962, a fibre glass shop was also included, as the use of glass fibre reinforced plastics came to be extensively used in body construction.

In 1962, planning permission was sought for further improvements to the Great Northern Road site, but this was refused on the ground that the property was affected' by proposals for major road works, involving the widening of Uttoxeter New Road. The Company appealed against refusal, but lost and made alternative plans to convert the running depot on the opposite side of the road into a new Central Works. This was completed early in 1968, and the original site was subsequently sold. The planned road improvements have never been carried out, and the site is occupied by a disused petrol filling station.

The new, 1924 depot was extended in 1929, to almost double its size. A number of houses around the depot were purchased and used as offices.

Following the completion of the major extensions at the Meadow Road depot, the whole of the allocation was transferred to Meadow Road on 20th March 1966. The depot was then used for a time as a dock shop, pending

An interior view of the building, taken around 1930-31, after conversion to a Central Works, and some of the vehicles are identifiable on the original print. Second from left is RA 6795, a Leyland bodied PLSC1 Lion acquired from Chapman of Belper in 1929. In the far corner is AL 8432, a Brush bodied Tilling Stevens acquired from Clayton of Nottingham in 1923, and by now converted to a Tillings B Type. Second from right is CH 4081, a Brush bodied Tilling Stevens TS6, and on the right is CH6231, a Brush bodied SOS Q of 1927

The 1924 Uttoxeter New Road depot, photographed in the mid sixties, with an Alexander bodied Tiger Cub on the forecourt. The high part of the building was the original, with the lower section on the left being the new extension added in 1929, creating a sizeable depot, able to hold around 120 vehicles at the time of construction, although this number had latterly reduced to about 70 with the increasing size of vehicles. On the right of the picture are some houses, nos. 27/29, Uttoxeter New Road, bought by the Company for use as offices. These were demolished In March 1966 to enable the construction of the new head office building shown on page 48. On conversion to a new Central Works, the external appearance from the road was not greatly altered, although the large doors were infilled, and a new door opening was created in the side that is obscured in this picture by the houses.

the conversion of the old Meadow Road depot to fulfill that function. From October that year, work took place to convert the depot to a new Central Works facility, and this was completed and transfer effected by March 1968.

The new Central Works was a modem, spacious facility including all the functions of the previous building, and also much new equipment. In particular, there was a new spray shop facility, enabling a change over from brush painting to spray. There was also equipment for reclaiming worn parts, in which the Company acquired considerable expertise. Although, with the addition of some of the North Western fleet in 1972, and the transfer of responsibility for Midland General vehicles in the same year, to be described in a subsequent volume, led to an increasing workload, the fleet size gradually reduced

from the mid nineteen seventies, and the Company began to take work in from outside, latterly marketing this capability under the name Trent Engineering.

Concurrently with these activities, the houses referred to above were demolished, and a new, four storey headquarters building was constructed, enabling the Traffic, Engineering and Secretarial functions to be housed under one roof for the first time. This is illustrated on page 48. In 1996, a start was made on relocating all the functions in the Uttoxeter New Road complex to the former Midland General Langley Mill depot and Head Office at Mansfield Road, Heanor, also to be described in a subsequent volume. The Head Office functions were relocated, to the former Midland General Head office building in 1996. The Uttoxeter New Road premises were subsequently sold for use as a self deposit facility, and the Company's 80 plus years connection with the site was severed.

When Uttoxeter New Road was an operational depot, it provided vehicles for all the Derby based services, in conjunction with Meadow Road depot.

DERBY BUS STATION

Trent's original Derby Bus Station was situated on the north side of Albert Street, opposite the Derby Co-op. It was amongst the earliest of bus stations, if not the first in the country, and the Company centralised its services there from on street stands at The Spot, Cheapside, Bold Lane and Albert Street. It was closed in 1933, when Trent transferred operations to the new municipal Central Bus Station in the Morledge. However, it was then taken over by Derby Corporation Omnibus Department, which used the area for parking off peak buses that were out of use during the day. It was demolished in the eighties, to make way for the present small shopping development.

Trent does not own the Central Bus Station, but it merits mention because the company was the principal user and rented offices there for the local traffic functions. This continued until 1986, when the office functions were relocated to Meadow Road depot, and services were re arranged to start and finish there. At that time, Derby City Transport began to make greater use of the facility in preparation for the anticipated loss of access to St Peters Street and The Spot due to pedestrianisation. However, the move of Trent services was unpopular with passengers and services once again began to call at the bus station in 1987, although continuing to start from Meadow Road. In 2000, the offices were once again relocated to the Bus Station, this time in the refurbished former cash office.

At the time of writing, the building is threatened with re-development, although there are moves in some quarters to have it preserved. Whilst for a utilitarian public building, it has considerable architectural merit (the designer, Charles Aslin was an eminent architect) and might have justified listing had it been adequately maintained, it is in less than perfect condition and was designed for shorter buses than the present 12m length vehicles. It is not, therefore, really suited to modern operating conditions, or the expectations of Trent's customers.

Albert Street, Derby, probably in the early 1930s. On the left is Trent's Bus Station, opened in 1922, and closed in 1933 when the new municipal Central Bus Station opened in The Morledge .

The new Municipal Central Bus Station in Derby, opened in 1933, and long the starting and finishing point for many Trent services over the years since. The Company rented offices from the Corporation on the central island platform shown, until 1986. They returned again in 2000, but the offices are now beyond the two storey section, off the right of the picture. Vehicles visible In this 1930s picture are Trent 122, CH 9902, a 1931 50S IM6 with Short body, on the right. The vehicle on the left, RB 4393, is a 1931 Morris Commercial Dictator of Eagle Bus service (S O Stevenson) of Little Eaton, later to become 1225 In the Trent fleet following takeover of part of the Eagle business in 1935.

HATTON DEPOT

Hatton depot is an outstation able to hold four vehicles, which was opened in 1942. Originally, its purpose was to house vehicles used on the local Burton services to Hatton and Rolleston, and to provide vehicles at the outer end of the Derby-Burton and Derby-Tutbury services. Today, it is used mainly for storage.

Hatton depot, photographed in 1999.

HUCKNALL DEPOT

Originally called Hucknall Torkard, after the Torkards who were Lords of the Manor, the main industry of Hucknall was coal mining. Indeed, for many years the depot stood in the shadow of the Sherwood Colliery winding gear, almost as a reminder of the principal industry of the area which it serves, but that has now gone following the reduction in the coal industry which took place in the 80s and 90s. Other industries, in addition to coal, were lace making, textiles, cabinet making and Rolls-Royce also have a manufacturing and testing facility there for aero engines.

Situated in Portland Road, the depot was opened on 10th March 1938, four buses having previously been kept at the adjoining Breedon and Wightman's garage. The Company first served Hucknall from August 1914, when a service was started between Nottingham and Mansfield, via Hucknall and Sutton in Ashfield. In 1929, the business of Reynolds Brothers was taken over, jointly with Nottingham Corporation, and this brought a Nottingham-Hucknall via Bulwell service. This was followed by the take-over of Dutton's Unity Service in 1935, which brought a number of services between Nottingham and Sutton in Ashfield, some of which was provided from Hucknall. With the growth of the business, especially following the Dutton take-over, there was a need to accommodate more buses in the town. Additional services were provided to the Ruffs and Beauvale estates, when these were developed after the war.

LOUGHBOROUGH DEPOT

The major industry in Loughborough is heavy mechanical and electrical engineering, Herbert Morris Ltd and the Brush Electrical Engineering Co Ltd being principal employers. The erstwhile Willowbrook factory was also in Loughborough and, as at many towns in the area, hosiery was an important industry. It is also a market town, home of Loughborough College and, nowadays, a University town.

Trent arrived in Loughborough in February 1919, as a result of the take-over of the Loughborough Road Car Co, Ltd. This acquisition brought with it a small garage at The Rushes, which had space for six vehicles, with open parking for three more behind. This provision was found satisfactory until 1934 when, owing to increased services, further buses were allocated to the depot, and all nine spaces were in use. The business of R E Horspool was taken over in October, 1935, bringing an additional four vehicles, and the take-over of the Sileby service, which Midland Red had recently acquired from J Squires was also in prospect. There was also an idea that the service of Howlett's of Quorn, on the same route, might be acquired but this, in the event, never materialised.

The adjoining site, previously used by a firm of weavers was acquired, and a new garage constructed on the entire site, being completed in 1937. Two adjoining houses were acquired in 1957, and a further extension brought into use on 1st September 1959, during the construction of which vehicles were

An April 2000 view of Hucknall depot.

The depot built by Trent on the site of the Loughborough Road Car Co premises in The Rushes, completed in 1937.

parked in the nearby British Waterways yard. Further improvements, in the form of a service lane, were carried out in the late sixties on land acquired by purchasing an adjoining shop premises.

From 2nd June 1986, five Midland Fox vehicles were out stationed at the depot. Subsequent events were to lead to the closure of the depot in July 1989, and the In January 1989, after a period of intense competition, to be described in a subsequent volume, Trent sold their Loughborough operation, and the subsequent events, which were to lead ultimately to its closure, in 1989 and subsequent demolition, in August 1990, will be described in a subsequent volume. The site now forms part of the car park of the adjacent Sainsbury's supermarket.

The final development of the Loughborough site by Trent, completed in the late sixties, the depot having also been extended in 1959.

MANSFIELD DEPOT

The original Mansfield depot was in Newgate Lane and had been used as a dormy shed for many years, having been acquired and modified in 1926. Land in Nursery Street Mansfield was bought from the Railway Executive in 1948, although negotiations went back to LMS Railway days, to build a new depot. The land was subject to a restrictive covenant, but this was lifted after recourse to the Official Arbitrator, which allowed the land to be used as required by the Company, but this was not taken forward, and the land was sold around 1960.

By 1957, the accommodation at Newgate Lane, which could hold only eight vehicles, was totally inadequate, and there was much duplicate mileage between Nottingham and Mansfield. However, East Midland were giving consideration at the time to extending their facilities in the town at Westgate, and decided in principle to do this and to offer Trent accommodation for 16 vehicles for the time being.

The East Midland depot extension was finished in 1958, and used by Trent for twelve vehicles from 14th September 1958, the garage in Newgate Lane, being sold soon afterwards. This additional capacity eliminated much dead mileage, and also eased the parking problems at Nottingham Manvers Street. This depot continued in use until October 1972. After this date, the vehicles were moved to the joint Mansfield District/Midland General depot at Sutton Road, Mansfield, but returned again in September, 1979. The depot closed in October 1984, and the various events leading up to this will be described in a subsequent volume

The former East Midland depot at Mansfield Westgate, which was shared by Trent until 1972, and then subsequently used from 1979 until 1984. Situated on the corner of Chesterfield Road South and Paulsfield Road, it is currently in use as a tyre and exhaust centre, as shown in this 2002 view.

MELBOURNE DEPOT

Melbourne is a small market town, where the Trent depot was acquired with the business of Higgs & Waller (Melbourne) Ltd in 1929. In 1947/8, alterations were carried out to raise the roof to accommodate double deckers and to provide accommodation for the Inspector in Charge, conductors' mess room and toilets. By 1992, the depot had become an out station of Meadow Road, but was closed in 1994, when the Melbourne services were handed over to Derby City Transport in exchange for those in Spondon - to be described in a subsequent volume. The site is now a supermarket.

A late fifties or early sixties photograph of the depot at Melbourne. Visible inside is 1355, JCH 355, one of the 1956 lowbridge Leyland PD2s, which was actually allocated to Shipley depot for the Ilkeston services, but which had found its way onto the Melbourne service, which also used lowbridge deckers. The saloon is one of the 1947/8 AEC Regals, probably 739, which was allocated to Melbourne.

NOTTINGHAM DEPOT

Nottingham is the East Midlands' premier city and built its original prosperity on lace making, pharmaceuticals, printing and engineering, as well as the Nottinghamshire coal field and other industries. The first Nottingham depot opened in February 1921, and was situated on Radford Marsh behind the White Horse public house in Ilkeston Road, where there was space to park twelve vehicles.

In 1926, a new depot was opened in Manvers Street on the corner of Stanhope Street, and this was used until the present depot was opened in 1933. The previous depot passed to Nottingham City Transport and still forms part of that company's Parliament Street depot to this day, albeit much altered and unrecognisable. In 1992, following the takeover of Barton in 1989, which will be described in a subsequent volume, the depot was re-designated as a Barton depot, and vehicles were transferred from Chilwell. For Trent vehicles, the depot became an out station, initially of Langley Mill, and then of Derby.

NOTTINGHAM (KENT STREET) DEPOT & HUNTINGDON HOUSE

This depot had been acquired with the business of Dutton's Unity Service in August 1935. During the war, in March 1941, it was requisitioned by the Air Ministry for the RAF and returned to the Company on 31st May 1946. In 1957, the staff canteen at the Huntingdon Street offices was relocated into Kent Street depot, in order to allow a new booking office to be provided on the corner of Kent Street and Huntingdon Street, and a centralised District Traffic Offices to be provided. The vehicles were transferred to Manvers Street depot. The depot had, in any event, only been used during the summer months, and was later sold.

Huntingdon House was the Company's main booking office in Nottingham, and also housed the local traffic and staff facilities, including the staff canteen. It was closed when Huntingdon Street Bus Station was closed in 1972.

Nottingham depot is a through building, with a one way system running from Lower Parliament Street to Manvers Street. The view, on the opposite page, taken in 1959 or 1960, shows a selection of contemporary vehicles, Tiger Cubs and PD2s, with a Royal Tiger coach hidden inside on the left, probably lined up for the annual Directors' visit.

The main Nottingham Traffic and Booking offices at Huntingdon House, on the corner of Huntingdon Street and Kent Street, Nottingham. The Kent Street depot is just visible on the left of the picture.

NOTTINGHAM (HUNTINGDON STREET) BUS STATION)

As with the Central Bus station at Derby, this was not a Trent owned facility, but was Council owned and operated, each operator paying the City Council departure charges for its use. Prior to it being opened in 1929, Trent vehicles (and others) had used on street stands. Trent made extensive use of the station until it closed in 1972. There were also two other bus stations in Nottingham. These were Broad Marsh, which Trent did not use during the BET years, and Mount Street. When the latter opened in 1943, Trent's services serving places to the west and north west of Nottingham were transferred there.

Nottingham's Huntingdon Street Bus Station in March 1932. Trent's SOSs are much in evidence near the top left of the picture. In the fore ground are mainly vehicles of Nottingham Corporation(as the NCT undertaking was then known), Barton and others. However, three Trent SOSs are evident immediately to the right of the Corporation double deck vehicle.

RIPLEY DEPOT

This was acquired with the business of A J Daley and Sons, Pippin Services in 1935. It was used operationally by Trent from then until October 1940, when the War Department commandeered it, for use as a workshop. When returned, it was not used by Trent, and, under an agreement dated 30th September 1947, was sold back to the Daleys.

Shipley depot - in the heart of Midland General/Notts & Derbys country. No Trent stage carriage services passed the door, but MGO's did! There is a story that one Trent driver entered the depot in a bit of a rush. He floored the brake pedal, but the floor was wet, and the bus skidded into the back wall! Possibly the single decker visible is 740, which spent much of it's time there, out of use as a spare. When withdrawn, it had a very low mileage.

SHIPLEY DEPOT

This depot, in the heart of Midland General country was situated at the junction of Hassock Lane with Pit Lane, next to the old Shipley Colliery. It was the only Trent depot situated away from the company's routes, and the doors were painted blue, allegedly to disguise it in Midland General's territory! From October 1940 until the end of the War, the Ministry of Aircraft Production requisitioned the building. It was closed in on 30th September 1972, when the allocation was transferred to Midland General's depot at Langley Mill, a few miles away, an event to be described in a subsequent volume.

The building was used for light industrial purposes for some years afterwards, but demolished in April 1998, in order to improve the appearance of the entrance to The American Adventure theme park, which had become established on the site of the adjacent former colliery. At the time of the transfer, only one of the original allocation of vehicles went to Langley Mill, the remaining vehicles being transferred from elsewhere.

An interior view of Shipley depot, taken in August 1972, shortly before closure, showing an Atlantean, Leopard and Fleetline. The blind on the Atlantean is set for the Ilkeston-Derby service, but it is a highbridge model, as by now Straws Bridge, in High Lane East, on the outskirts of Ilkeston, which required the use of low height deckers, on this service, had been demolished. This followed closure of the railway line, in 1964.

SKEGNESS BOOKING OFFICE

Trent began its first express service, to Skegness, in 1922, and it remained a firm favourite for many years. The Company maintained this booking office in Lumley Street from an early stage, possibly until the Skegness service was suspended during the war, or possibly until the early fifties, when a converted 1935 SOS DON bus came into use as a booking office. In turn, the bus was replaced in the sixties by a caravan, which was towed to and from Skegness by a Land Rover at the start and end of the summer season.

The Booking Office in Lumley Road, Skegness.

SOUTH NORMANTON DEPOT

This was acquired with the business of E Naylor & Sons in July 1956. It was used for several years, but by October 1961 was considered to be in a poor state of repair and was sold. It operated as an outstation of Alfreton depot, and buses carried yellow numberplates.

This view of the future 645, PRB 709, new in 1953, provides just a glimpse of Naylor's South Normanton depot prior to the Trent take over. It was an AEC Regal IV and became a unique vehicle when it joined the Trent fleet, although the the Burlingham Seagull coachwork fitted in quite readily at Trent.

WIRKSWORTH DEPOT

Wirksworth is a small town that owes much of its existence to quarrying. Trent acquired the depot, on the Idridgehay road in the outskirts of the town, with the business of Rhodeland Motor Services of Derby in 1933. Around 1946, it was extended, and also the roof was raised to enable double deckers to be accommodated. It was closed in the mid seventies, probably because the 1972 takeover of North Western, to be described in a subsequent volume, brought the Company a depot at Matlock, and enabled the linking of previously separate services. The building was later sold, but still stands, and is used for industrial purposes.

Wirksworth depot was closed in the seventies, and is now used for industrial purposes, as shown by this 2002 view.

Depot Codes used to indicate Vehicle Allocation.				
Depot	Type of code displayed on vehicle			
	Colour backing to fleetnumber plate	Colour sticker on windscreen	Colour transfer alongside fleet number transfer	Letter transfers alongside fleetnumber transfer *
Alfreton	Yellow	Yellow	Yellow	AL
Ashbourne	Red/black	Silver	Silver	AS
Belper	Black	Black	Black	B
Castle Donington	Code not used - depot closed.			
Derby (Meadow Road)	Brown	Brown	Brown	D
Derby (Uttoxeter New	Red	Pink	Red	Closed as a depot.
Hatton	Red	Pink	Red	HA
Hucknall	Orange	Orange	Black	HU
Loughborough	Blue	Blue	Orange	L
Mansfield	Red/Green	Light Green	Green	MD
Melbourne	Red/White	Gold	Red or Brown	M
Nottingham (Manvers Street)	Green	Dark Green	Gold	N
Nottingham (Kent Street)	Green	Not used - Depot closed.		
Ripley	Code not used - depot sold in 1946.			
Shipley	White	White	Red or Brown	Closed
South Normanton	Yellow	Not used - depot sold		
Wirksworth	As for Derby depots			W

* After a fairly short period, the letter codes ceased to be displayed on vehicles, although the same codes continued to be used for administration purposes, and some were later changed.

Ancillary Vehicles

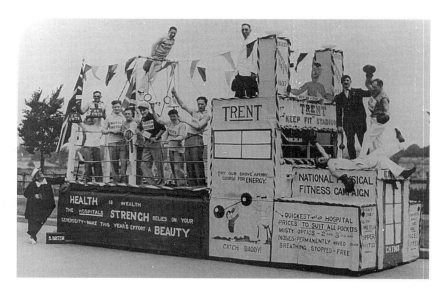

Bus 802 an SOS FS, new in 1926, but acquired from Midland Red in 1935, was converted to the first driver training vehicle 15 in 1937. In this form it was, for some reason, known as the "chocolate box"and remained in use until 1952.

The replacement for the chocolate box was no 22, originally bus 363, a 1936 SOS DON, converted by Central Works in 1952. It remained in use until the sixties.

A Tilling Stevens TS3 bus chassis supports this carnival float! Bus D134, new in 1920 was withdrawn in 1928 and converted by the Company for use as a general purpose lorry. It also carried a variety of designs when used by staff for a carnival float.

There were other buses converted into lorries, of which photographs have not been found. However, the last to be so treated was 751, a 1946 AEC Regal. After withdrawal in 1959, Central Works built this modern looking coach built cab using grille and front bumper from current AEC goods models, and added the open lorry body for general purpose use.

This ex War department Canadian GMC, No 21, was acquired by the Company in 1947 and converted to a breakdown tender. It was sent to Frank Cowley, the dealer, on the Chief Engineer's instructions after breaking down itself when going to recover a broken down vehicle!

Below is the tree cutter known as "King Kong", which had a remarkable history. An SOS IM4 new as bus no 263 in 1933, it was soon fitted with a Gardner 4LW diesel engine, being the Company's first diesel engine vehicle. It spent its latter days out stationed at Wirksworth depot, because it was known as an unfailing starter, but after 287, 725 miles on service it was withdrawn and converted to a tree cutting vehicle.

A newer vehicle acquired for vehicle recovery was this ex Forces AEC Matador, always a popular choice with bus operators, and Central Works coachbuilt a new body for it.

In this photograph, the Matador above is being used for training in recovery of an overturned vehicle without causing damage. The "overturned" vehicle is 1219, a former Naylors AEC Regent III.

Fleet Numbering System

The first few vehicles carried no fleet numbers, so far as is known, but with the arrival of the first Maudslays, a series of numbers was introduced starting at D100, and these were sign written on the chassis frames. The meaning of D is not known, but it has been suggested that may have stood for Derby, at a time when BET Secretarial work was carried out centrally in London. The Maudslays were soon sold to the War Office, and when the replacement Tilling Stevens arrived, they - started the system again at D100. In the early twenties, the ex War Department Thornycrofts were given numbers in series with the Tilling Stevens, but prefixed T. Similarly, the four Vulcans that arrived at about the same time were also numbered in series, but with a prefix V.

In 1923, Mr G C Campbell-Taylor arrived as General Manager and introduced a new system based on blocks of numbers for different vehicle types. This is a fairly common idea in the industry, and although the tidiness of the system has varied over the years, is still the basis of the system used by the Company today. The unusual facet of Mr Campbell-Taylor's approach, however, was the introduction of colour coding to indicate the depot to which each vehicle was allocated. The fleet number was carried on an embossed plate screwed to the vehicle, usually on the bonnet, on the cab side and on the lower rear panel, although in the late fifties an additional plate was added on the front, as well. The colour code was painted onto the number plate as a background to the raised numbers. If a vehicle was transferred to a different depot, then the number plates had to be painted in the colour code for the receiving depot.

In 1962, it was decided that the fleet numbering, which extended up to 1373, had become untidy, and most vehicles were then renumbered, with the object of bringing all numbers below 1000, and re-affirming the blocks of numbers used for each type. This has the advantage that staff and management can more easily know the type of vehicle from its fleet number.

At the same time, the colour plate system was abandoned, and vehicles at first carried a small plastic number plate in cream with orange edging and the number in black. After a fairly short period, new number plates, of similar size but in yellow plastic with the number printed on in black were introduced. Again, these were short lived and the numbers were then marked using transfers in yellow or gold with black edging. This continued to the end of the BET era, and, indeed, continues today, although the colour of the numerals has varied from time to time. A list of the colour codes for each depot can be found on page 139.

Pre-war numberplate, in pressed brass and colour coded.

Plastic number plate used in 1962 renumbering scheme

Post-war numberplate, in pressed aluminium and colour coded.

Fleet number applied with transfers from mid- sixties.

Fleet List - 1946-67.

Year to Stock	Fleet No	Registration No	Chassis	Body	Layout	Year W'drwn.	Remarks (Rb - Rebodied, Rn - Renumbered)	Add'l Note
1946	637-42	RC 8740-6	AEC Regal I 0662	Duple	C31F	1956		1
1946	720	RC 8747	AEC Regal I 0662	Willow brook	B34F	1960	Rn 730, 1959	
1946	721	RC 8748	AEC Regal I 0662	Willow brook	B34F	1959		
1946	722-3	RC 8749-50	AEC Regal I 0662	Willow brook	B34F	1960	Rn 732/4, 1959	
1946	724-5	RC 8751-2	AEC Regal I 0662	Willow brook	B34F	1959		
1946	1117-29	RC 8915-27	AEC Regent II 0661	Willow brook	H54R	1960		
1946	726	RC 8992	AEC Regal I 0662	Willow brook	B34F	1959		
1946	727	RC 8993	AEC Regal I 0662	Willow brook	B34F	1960	Rn 736, 1959	
1946	728-48	RC 8994-9014	AEC Regal I 0662	Willow brook	B34F	1959-60		
1946	749	RC 9015	AEC Regal I 0662	Willow brook	B34F	1960	Rn 739, 1959	
1946	750	RC 9016	AEC Regal I 0662	Willow brook	B34F	1960	Rn 743, 1959	
1946	751	RC 9017	AEC Regal I 0662	Willow brook	B34F	1959	Converted to lorry 19, withdrawn 1965	
1947	1130-41	RC 9646-57	AEC Regent II 0661	Willow brook	H56R	1960		
1947	752	RC 9658	AEC Regal I 0662	Willow brook	B35F	1963	Rn 301, rebuilt FDP39F, 1958	
1947	753-6	RC 9659-62	AEC Regal I 0662	Willow brook	B35F	1960		
1947	757	RC 9663	AEC Regal I 0662	Willow brook	B35F	1963	Rn 300, rebuilt FDP39F, 1958	
1947	758	RC 9664	AEC Regal I 0662	Willow brook	B35F	1960		
1947	759	RC 9665	AEC Regal I 0662	Willow brook	B35F	1962	Rn 302, rebuilt FDP39F, 1958	
1947	760-1	RC 9666-7	AEC Regal I 0662	Willow brook	B35F	1960		
1947	762	RC 9668	AEC Regal I 0662	Willow brook	B35F	1963	Rn 303, rebuilt FDP39F, 1958	
1947	763-4	RC 9669-70	AEC Regal I 0662	Willow brook	B35F	1960		
1947	765	RC 9671	AEC Regal I 0662	Willow brook	B35F	1962	Rn 304, rebuilt FDP39F, 1958	
1947	766-8	RC 9672-4	AEC Regal I 0662	Willow brook	B35F	1960		
1947	769	RC 9675	AEC Regal I 0662	Willow brook	B35F	1962	Rn 305, rebuilt FDP39F, 1958	
1947	770	RC 9676	AEC Regal I 0662	Willow brook	B35F	1960		
1947	771	RC 9677	AEC Regal I 0662	Willow brook	B35F	1962	Rn 306, rebuilt FDP39F, 1958	
1947	772	RC 9678	AEC Regal I 0662	Willow brook	B35F	1962	Rn 307, rebuilt FDP39F, 1958	
1947	773	RC 9679	AEC Regal I 0662	Willow brook	B35F	1960		
1947	774	RC 9680	AEC Regal I 0662	Willow brook	B35F	1963	Rn 308, rebuilt FDP39F, 1958	
1947	775	RC 9681	AEC Regal I 0662	Willow brook	B35F	1962	Rn 309, rebuilt FDP39F, 1958	
1947	776	RC 9682	AEC Regal I 0662	Willow brook	B35F	1960	Rn 752, 1959	
1947	777	RC 9683	AEC Regal I 0662	Willow brook	B35F	1963	Rn 310, rebuilt FDP39F, 1958	
1947	778	RC 9684	AEC Regal I 0662	Willow brook	B35F	1960	Rn 757, 1959	
1947	779	RC 9685	AEC Regal I 0662	Willow brook	B35F	1962	Rn 311, rebuilt FDP39F, 1958	
1947	780	RC 9686	AEC Regal I 0662	Willow brook	B35F	1960	Rn 759, 1959	
1947	781	RC 9687	AEC Regal I 0662	Willow brook	B35F	1963	Rn 312, rebuilt FDP39F, 1958	
1947	782	RC 9688	AEC Regal I 0662	Willow brook	B35F	1960	Rn 762, 1959	
1947	783	RC 9689	AEC Regal I 0662	Willow brook	B35F	1962	Rn 313, rebuilt FDP39F, 1958	
1947	784	RC 9690	AEC Regal I 0662	Willow brook	B35F	1960	Rn 765, 1959	
1947	785	RC 9691	AEC Regal I 0662	Willow brook	B35F	1960	Rn 769, 1959	

Year to Stock	Fleet No	Registration No	Chassis	Body	Layout	Year W'drwn.	Remarks (Rb - Rebodied, Rn - Renumbered)	Add'l Note
1947	786-8	RC 9692-4	AEC Regal I O662	Willow brook	B35F	1962-3	Rn 314-6, rebuilt FDP39F, 1958	
1947	789	RC 9695	AEC Regal I O662	Willow brook	B35F	1960	Rn 771, 1959	
1947	790	RC 9696	AEC Regal I O662	Willow brook	B35F	1963	Rn 317, rebuilt FDP39F, 1958	
1947	791	RC 9697	AEC Regal I O662	Willow brook	B35F	1960	Rn 772, 1959	
1947	792	RC 9698	AEC Regal I O662	Willow brook	B35F	1963	Rn 318, rebuilt FDP39F, 1958	
1947	793	RC 9699	AEC Regal I O662	Willow brook	B35F	1962	Rn 319, rebuilt FDP39F, 1958	
1947	794	RC 9700	AEC Regal I O662	Willow brook	B35F	1960	Rn 774, 1959	
1948	600-11	ACH 430-41	AEC Regal III O682	Windover	C32F	1959	600-7 C30F, prior to 1953	2
1948	1142-61	ACH 632-51	AEC Regent II O661	Willow brook	H56R	1962-3		
1948	1320-9	ACH 652-61	AEC Regent II O661	Willow brook	L55R	1963		
1949			No vehicles received					
1950	100-19	BRC 300-19	AEC Regal III 6821X	Willow brook	DP33F	1961		3
1950	1200-9	BRC 400-9	AEC Regent III 9612X	Willow brook	H56R	1964	Rn 700-9 , 1962	3
1951	1220-5	CCH 620-5	Leyland Titan PD2/3	Leyland	H56R	1964	Rn 710-5, 1962	4
1951	200-9	CRC 510-9	Leyland Royal Tiger PSU1/15	Leyland	C41C	1961-2		
1952	1226-35	CRC 826-35	Leyland Titan PD2/12	Leyland	H58R	1964	Rn 716-25, 1962	
1952	800-9	DCH 900-9	Leyland Royal Tiger PSU1/7	Leyland	B44F	1962	Rn 350-9, 1962	
1953	1236-50	DRC 936-50	Leyland Titan PD2/12	Leyland	H58RD	1965-67	Rn 726-40, 1962	
1953	210-1	ECH 210-1	Leyland Royal Tiger PSU1/15	Willow brook	C37C	1963-4	Rn4-5, 1962	
1953	212	ECH 212	Leyland R. Tiger PSU1/15	Willow brook	C37C	1964	Rn12, then 6, 1962	
1953	213-5	ECH 213-5	Leyland R. Tiger PSU1/15	Willow brook	C37C	1963	Rn7-9, 1962	
1954	810-19	FCH 10-19	Leyland Tiger Cub PSUC1/1	Saro	B44F	1965	Rn 360-9, 1962	
1954	820-9	FCH 20-9	Leyland Tiger Cub PSUC1/1	Weymann	B44F	1965	Rn 370-9, 1962	
1954	120	GCH 120	Leyland Tiger Cub PSUC1/2T	Willow brook	DP41F	1969	Commercial Motor Show exhibit, 1954	
1955	1251-6	FRC 951-6	Leyland Titan PD2/12	Leyland	H58RD	1962	Rn 741-6, 1962	5
1955	121-9	GRC 121-9	Leyland Tiger Cub PSUC1/2T	Willow brook	DP41F	1966-8		
1955	130-9	GRC 130-9	Leyland Tiger Cub PSUC1/2T	Weymann	DP41F	1964-7		
1955	216-21	GRC 216-21	Leyland Tiger Cub PSUC1/2T	Burlingham Seagull	C37F	1964-6	Rn16-21, 1962	
1955	140-51	HRC 140-51	Leyland Tiger Cub PSUC1/2T	Willow brook	DP41F	1966-7		
1956	1257-66	JCH 257-66	Leyland Titan PD2/12	Metro Cammell	H59RD	1967-8	Rn 747-56, 1962	
1956	1352-7	JCH 352-7	Leyland Titan PD2/12	Metro Cammell	L55RD	1967-8	Rn 694-9, 1962	
1956	643	NNU 648	AEC Regal III 9621A	Burlingham	C33F	1959	Ex Naylor, South Normanton, new 1949	
1956	644	ORA 181	AEC Regal III 9621E	Burlingham	FC33F	1959	Ex Naylor, South Normanton, new 1950	
1956	645	PRB 709	AEC Regal IV 9821E	Burlingham Seagull	C37C	1961	Ex Naylor, South Normanton, new 1951	
1956	646	XRB 50	AEC Reliance MU3RV	Burlingham Seagull	C37C	1963	Ex Naylor, South Normanton, new 1955 Rn 8, then 10, 1962	
1956	647	XRB 51	AEC Reliance MU3RV	Burlingham Seagull	C37C	1963	Ex Naylor, South Normanton, new 1955 Rn 9, then 11, 1962	
1956	1216	JNU 796	Guy Arab II 5LW	Strachan	L55R	1959	Ex Naylor, South Normanton, new 1945 Rn 1300, 1956	
1956	1217	MNU 777	Guy Arab III 6LW	NCB	H56R	1959	Ex Naylor, South Normanton, new 1948	

144

Year to Stock	Fleet No	Registration No	Chassis	Body	Layout	Year W'drwn.	Remarks (Rb - Rebodied, Rn - Renumbered)	Add'l Note
1956	1218	VO 8566	AEC Regent 661	Burlingham	H56R	1959	Ex Naylor, South Normanton, new 1932 (chassis), 1949 (body and 7.7litre diesel engine).Chassis ex Mansfield District 66.	
1956	1219	MRB 709	AEC Regent III 0961	Brush	H56R	1960	Ex Naylor, South Normanton, new 1948	
1957	1000-7	KCH 100-7	Leyland Titan PD2/12	Metro Cammell	H59RD	1968-9	Rn 757-64, 1962	
1957	1008	KCH 108	Leyland Titan PD2/12	Metro Cammell	H59RD	1976/ 1977	Rn 765, 1962. Rn 589, 1974. Reinstated following fire, 1976.	
1957	1009	KCH 109	Leyland Titan PD2/12	Metro Cammell	H59RD	1969	Rn 766 , 1962	
1957	1010	KCH 110	Leyland Titan PD2/12	Metro Cammell	H59RD	1972&77	Rn 767, 1962. Rn 590, 1974.	
1957	1011	KCH 111	Leyland Titan PD2/12	Metro Cammell	H59RD	1969	Rn 768, 1962	
1957	1012	KCH 112	Leyland Titan PD2/12	Metro Cammell	H59RD	1972 & 77	Rn 769, 1962. Rn 591, 1974.	
1957	1013-21	KCH 113-21	Leyland Titan PD2/12	Metro Cammell	H59RD	1968-71	Rn 770-8, 1962	
1957	1022	KCH 122	Leyland Titan PD2/12	Metro Cammell	H59RD	1973,76 & 1977	Rn 779, 1962. Rn 592, 1974. Reinstated following fire, 1976.	
1957	1023-5	KCH 123-5	Leyland Titan PD2/12	Metro Cammell	H59RD	1968-9	Rn 780-2, 1962	
1957	1026	KCH 126	Leyland Titan PD2/12	Metro Cammell	H59RD	1973,76 & 1977	Rn 783, 1962. Rn 593, 1974. Reinstated following fire, 1976.	
1957	1027-33	KCH 127-33	Leyland Titan PD2/12	Metro Cammell	H59RD	1968-71	Rn 784-90, 1962	
1957	222-8	KCH 222-8	Leyland Tiger Cub PSUC1/2T	Burlingham Seagull	C37C	1965-6	Rn 22-8, 1962	
1958	1034-51	LRC 434-51	Leyland Titan PD3/4	Willowbrook	H73RD	1971	Rn 400-17, 1962	
1958	1052	LRC 452	Leyland Titan PD3/4	Willowbrook	H73RD	1972, 76 & 77	Rn 418, 1962. Rn 586, 1972. Reinstated following fire, 1976	
1958	1053	LRC 453	Leyland Titan PD3/4	Willowbrook	H73RD	1972, 73, 76 & 77	Rn 419, 1962. Rn 587, 1972. Reinstated following fire, 1976	
1958	1054	LRC 454	Leyland Titan PD3/4	Willowbrook	H73RD	1972 & 1977	Rn 420, 1962, rn 588, 1972. Conv to training vehicle A54, 1977. Pres'rv'd 1987	
1958	1055	LRC 455	Leyland Titan PD3/4	Willowbrook	H73RD	1971	Rn 421, 1962	
1959	152-61	NRC 152-61	Leyland Tiger Cub PSUC1/2	Willowbrook	DP41F	1968	Rn 350-9, 1962. Altered to B45F, 1965	
1959	1056-9	ORC 656-9	Leyland Atlantean PDR1/1	Metro Cammell	H78F	1972-3	Rn 422-5, 1962, 589-92, 1972.	
1959	1060-4	ORC 660-4	Leyland Atlantean PDR1/1	Metro Cammell	H78F	1972	Rn 426-30, 1962, 428 Rn 595, 1972.	
1959	1065	ORC 665	Leyland Atlantean PDR1/1	Metro Cammell	H78F	1972	Rn 431, 1962. Rn 598, 1972.	
1959	1066	ORC 666	Leyland Atlantean PDR1/1	Metro Cammell	H78F	1972	Rn 432, 1962	
1959	1358-67	ORC 758-67	Leyland Atlantean PDR1/1	Weymann	L73F	1972-3	Rn 600-9, 1962	
1959	1368	ORC 768	Leyland Atlantean PDR1/1	Weymann	L73F	1977	Rn 610, 1962	
1960	1067-8	RRC 67-8	Leyland Atlantean PDR1/1	Roe	H78F	1973-4	Rn 433-4, 1962	
1960	1069	RRC 69	Leyland Atlantean PDR1/1	Roe	H78F	1975	Rn 435, 1962	
1960	1070	RRC 70	Leyland Atlantean PDR1/1	Roe	H78F	1972	Rn 436, 1962+I193.	
1960	1071-7	RRC 71-7	Leyland Atlantean PDR1/1	Roe	H78F	1972-3	Rn 437-43, 1962	
1960	1078	RRC 78	Leyland Atlantean PDR1/1	Roe	H78F	1975	Rn 444, 1962	
1960	1079	RRC 79	Leyland Atlantean PDR1/1	Roe	H78F	1973	Rn 445, 1962	
1960	1080	RRC 80	Leyland Atlantean PDR1/1	Roe	H78F	1977	Rn 446, 1962,464, 1976, 598, 1977.	
1960	1081	RRC 81	Leyland Atlantean PDR1/1	Roe	H78F	1974	Rn 447, 1962	

Year to Stock	Fleet No	Registration No	Chassis	Body	Layout	Year W'drwn.	Remarks (Rb - Rebodied, Rn - Renumbered)	Add'l Note
1960	1082-3	RRC 82-3	Leyland Atlantean PDR1/1	Roe	H78F	1972	Rn 448-9, 1962	
1960	1084	RRC 84	Leyland Atlantean PDR1/1	Roe	H78F	1973	Rn 450, 1962	
1960	1085-6	RRC 85-6	Leyland Atlantean PDR1/1	Roe	H78F	1975	Rn 451-2, 1962	
1960	1087-9	RRC 87-9	Leyland Atlantean PDR1/1	Roe	H78F	1972	Rn 453-5, 1962	
1960	229-32	RRC 229-32	AEC Reliance 2MU3RA	Weymann Fanfare	C37F	1967	Rn 29-32, 1962, 40-3, 1964	
1960	233	RRC 233	AEC Reliance 2MU3RA	Weymann Fanfare	C37F	1970	Rn 33, 1962, 50, 1964 Rb Harrington C37F, 1962	
1960	234-8	RRC 234-8	AEC Reliance 2MU3RA	Weymann Fanfare	C37F	1966-7	Rn 34-8, 1962	
1960	1369	SRC 369	Leyland Atlantean PDR1/1	Weymann	L73F	1977	Rn 611 , 1962	
1960	1370-3	SRC 370-3	Leyland Atlantean PDR1/1	Weymann	L73F	1974	Rn 612-5, 1962	
1960	1090	TCH 90	Leyland Atlantean PDR1/1	Roe	H78F	1977	Rn 456, 1962, 472, 1976, 599, 1977.	
1960	1091	TCH 91	Leyland Atlantean PDR1/1	Roe	H78F	1974	Rn 457, 1962	
1960	1092	TCH 92	Leyland Atlantean PDR1/1	Roe	H78F	1972	Rn 458, 1962. Commercial Motor Show exhibit, 1960.	
1960	1093-4	TCH 93-4	Leyland Atlantean PDR1/1	Roe	H78F	1972	Rn 459-60, 1962	
1960	1095	TCH 95	Leyland Atlantean PDR1/1	Roe	H78F	1973	Rn 461, 1962	
1961	162-76	VCH 162-76	Leyland Tiger Cub PSUC1/2	Willow brook	DP41F	1970-1		
1961	39-42	VCH 239-42	AEC Reliance 2MU3RA	Burlingham Seagull 70	C41F	1968	Rn 44-8, 1964	6
1961	830-44	VCH 830-44	Leyland Tiger Cub PSUC1/1	Willow brook	B45F	1975-6	Rn 380, 1962	
1962	43-6	YRC 43-6	AEC Reliance 2MU3RA	Harrington Cavalier	C37F	1970	Rn 51-4, 1963	
1962	177-96	YRC 177-96	Leyland Tiger Cub PSUC1/1	Alexander	DP41F	1975-77	191 re-acquired for preservation, 1988 194 converted to training vehicle A54.	
1962	462-3	62-3 ACH	Leyand Atlantean PDR1/1	Weymann	H77F	1977	Rn 577/8, 1977	
1962	464	64 ACH	Leyland Atlantean PDR1/1	Weymann	H77F	1976	Destroyed by fire.	
1962	465-71	65-71 ACH	Leyand Atlantean PDR1/1	Weymann	H77F	1977-8	Rn 580-5, 1977	
1963	200-23	200-23 CCH	Leyland Leopard PSU3/1R	Willow brook	DP51F	1977-8	204,20-1 destroyed by fire, 1976. 201 converted to training vehicle A59.	
1963	616-25	616-25 CCH	Daimler Fleetline CRG6LX	Northern Counties	H77F	1977-8	622 destroyedby fire, 1976	
1963	1-3	121-3 FCH	Leyland Leopard PSU3/3RT	Plaxton Panorama	C49F	1973	1 delivered as ACH 1B	
1964	55-9	ACH 55-9B	Leyland Leopard L2	Harrington Grenadier	C40F	1976	Reseated C41F, 1970	
1964	224-31	ACH 224-31B	Leyland Leopard PSU3/1RT	Alexander	C49F	1978	231 used as training vehicle A59	
1964	300-7	ACH 300--7B	Leyland Leopard PSU3/1	Marshall	B53F	1978-80	Operated as B45F 1968/69. 303 destroyed by fire, 1976.304 used as training vehicle A60.	
1964	308-15	ACH 308-15B	Leyland Leopard PSU3/1	Marshall	B53F	1979-80	313 damaged by fire, 1976.	
1965	4-7	ECH 4-7C	Leyland Leopard PSU3/3RT	Plaxton Panorama	C49F	1973		
1965	70-5	ECH 70-5C	Bedford SB5	Duple Bella Vista	C41F	1971		
1965	232-40	ECH 232-40C	Leyland Leopard PSU3/1R	Willow brook	DP49F	1980	234 altered to B49F, 1980.	
1965	241	ECH 241C	Leyland Leopard PSU3/1R	Willow brook	DP49F	1977		
1965	242-51	ECH 242-51C	Leyland Leopard PSU3/1R	Willow brook	DP51F	1978-80	245 destroyed by fire.1976.	
1965	472	ECH 472C	Daimler Fleetline CRG6LX	Alexander	H78F	1976	Destroyed by fire.	

Year to Stock	Fleet No	Registration No	Chassis	Body	Layout	Year W'drwn.	Remarks (Rb - Rebodied, Rn - Renumbered)	Add'l Note
1965	473-81	ECH 473-81C	Daimler Fleetline CRG6LX	Alexander	H78F	1979-81	Rn 973-981, 1977	
1965	100	HRC 100C	Leyland Tiger Cub PSUC1/11	Alexander	C41F	1978		
1965	101	HRC 101C	Leyland Tiger Cub PSUC1/11	Alexander	C41F	1980		
1965	102-7	HRC 102-7C	Leyland Tiger Cub PSUC1/11	Alexander	C41F	1979-80		
1966	482-9	HRC 482-9D	Daimler Fleetline CRG6LX	Alexander	H77F	1978-80	Rn 982-9, 1978	
1966	490	HRC 490D	Daimler Fleetline CRG6LX	Alexander	H77F	1977	Destroyed by fire, Dec 1977.	
1966	491	HRC 491D	Daimler Fleetline CRG6LX	Alexander	H77F	1978	Rn 991, 1978	
1966	60-2	JCH 60-2D	Leyland Leopard L2	Plaxton Panorama	C40F	1977		
1966	252	JRC 252D	Leyland Leopard PSU3/3R	Metro-Cammell	DP51F	1978		
1966	253	JRC 253D	Leyland Leopard PSU3/3R	Metro-Cammell	DP51F	1980		
1966	254-61	JRC 254-61D	Leyland Leopard PSU3/3R	Metro-Cammell	DP51F	1977-8		
1967	492-99	MRC 492-99E	Daimler Fleetline CRG6LX	Alexander	H77F	1978-9	Rn 992-9, 1978	
1967	500	MRC 500E	Daimler Fleetline CRG6LX	Alexander	H77F	1979	Rn 900, 1978	
1967	501	MRC 501E	Daimler Fleetline CRG6LX	Alexander	H77F	1976	Destroyed by fire.	
1967	502	MRC 502E	Daimler Fleetline CRG6LX	Alexander	H77F	1980	Rn 902, 1978	
1967	503	MRC 503E	Daimler Fleetline CRG6LX	Alexander	H77F	1981	Rn 903, 1978. To training vehicle	
1967	504	MRC 504E	Daimler Fleetline CRG6LX	Alexander	H77F	1976	Destroyed by fire.	
1967	505-7	MRC 505-7E	Daimler Fleetline CRG6LX	Alexander	H77F	1980-1	Rn 905-7, 1978	
1967	508	MRC 508E	Daimler Fleetline CRG6LX	Alexander	H77F	1978	Rn 908, 1978	
1967	509	MRC 509E	Daimler Fleetline CRG6LX	Alexander	H77F	1981	Rn 909, 1978	
1967	510	MRC 510E	Daimler Fleetline CRG6LX	Alexander	H77F	1979	Rn 910, 1978	
1967	511	MRC 511E	Daimler Fleetline CRG6LX	Alexander	H77F	1980	Rn 911, 1978	
1967	512	MRC 512E	Daimler Fleetline CRG6LX	Alexander	H77F	1976	Destroyed by fire.	
1967	63-7	MRC 563-7E	Leyland Leopard PSU4/3R	Plaxton Panorama	C40F	1978-9		
1967	76-81	MRC 576-81E	Bedford VAM5	Duple Viceroy	C41F	1972	79 destroyed by fire, 1972.	
1967	8-11	PRC 208-11F	Leyland Leopard PSU3/4R	Plaxton Panorama	C49F	1978		

This list has been compiled largely from Company records, although with the assistance of the records of the PSV Circle, which is hereby acknowledged.

Readers with a particular interest in vehicles are commended to join the PSV Circle, which is the national enthusiast body for vehicle records.

Additional Notes referred to on pages 143 to 147

Note	Remarks
1	AEC Regal II. Although the chassis of these vehicles were new, the bodies were used, having been removed from 1938 Daimler COG5/40 chassis, 637-42, RC5987-93, in 1942 and stored for the duration of the war.
2	AEC Regal III. 608/9 were C29F during the winter, from 1949. 611 is preserved.
3	AEC Regal III, and AEC Regent III. These vehicles were fitted with Crossley syncromesh gearboxes, as indicated by the X in the chassis designation, and were the only examples of the two models so fitted. They were also the first 8ft wide vehicles supplied
4	Leyland Titan PD2/3. It is said that these vehicles were a diverted order, possibly from Newcastle Corporation, but no evidence has been found to in either Trent or Leyland records, which both indicate that the order was placed by Trent.
5	Leyland Titan PD2/12. This batch of vehicles had the last bus bodies built at Leyland's Farington Works. The last of the batch, 1256, is preserved.
6	AEC Reliance. 45 was fitted with a ZF six-speed syncromesh gearbox from new.

Huntingdon Street Holiday Happenings

A particular feature of Trent operations during the BET years was the large number of seaside express services, which began with a service from Nottingham to Skegness in 1922. These expanded considerably and at peak times, particularly when the factories had their summer holiday close down, all manner of vehicles had to be hired to supplement the Company's own fleet and cope with the traffic. Times have changed, and the seaside holiday has been replaced by the package holiday abroad, whilst the modern Trent concentrates firmly on running local bus services. This fascinating selection of views provides an insight into a previous era.

This marvellous view, taken by Geoff Atkins in August 1931, captures the crowded atmosphere as SOS QC 604 with Carlyle body loads at a Huntingdon Street looking rather different from the present day. Visible on the left is a door of the Company van, used to convey luggage, whilst on the right is a Tansey and Severn Leyland TD1, in the bus station, on the stand for Alfreton.

1929 SOS Madam 424, CH 8124, looks set for a good load, but the weather was poor in this atmospheric shot taken in August 1931. Everyone is wrapped up warm, and how about the cloche hats for a fashion statement!

The Wass Bros business was sold to East Midland in the fifties, but in August 1938, they were running this Leyland Lion LT5B with Willowbrook 32seat coach body which Trent was able to hire.

148

This Leyland Comet CPO1 with Strachan C37F coachwork was a rare vehicle indeed, being one of a batch of five supplied in 1951 to Homeland Tours of Croydon, which were the only 30ft long Comets ever built. HRK 905 was in the fleet of A Fenwick of Old Bolingbroke near Spilsby when hired to Trent for duplication on the Mablethorpe service.

F, T & Mrs R Butler's stage carriage service between Kirkby in Ashfield and Annesley Woodhouse was sold to Trent in 1935, but the firm continues in business as Butler Bros, mainly as a coach operator, and was able to hire this 1951 Leyland Tiger PS2 with Yeates FC37F body, MAL 386, to Trent to help out in taking holiday makers to Cleethorpes.

Roy's of Mapperley, Nottingham, provided this Leyland Tiger PS1 with unusual Harrington FC39F body, HTJ 617, for service to Mablethorpe. The vehicle had originally been new to Kenilworth Tours of Liverpool. Roy's eventually sold their business to Skills.

This Roe bodied Daimler Freeline 18, AEX 18B, of Great Yarmouth Corporation was fairly unusual, both because the Freeline chassis was rare, and because municipal operators tended not to operate outside their boundaries in August 1965, when this view was taken. The vehicle features high backed seats, so the passengers probably had a fairly comfortable ride.

Postscript to Part One

Some additional information has come to hand since the publication of Part One, including the photographs shown on this page, and the two items below:

Page 142: D137, CH 1977 was renumbered 51 by 12/26, not 52 as shown.
Page 154: The vehicle used as a booking office and subsequently preserved was 321, RC 2721, not as shown.

This photograph shows London Transport RT 19 operating for Trent as a demonstrator in 1942 - note the "On hire to Trent" label above the bonnet. Although Trent placed orders in 1943 for further AECs for post war delivery, it is not known whether RT 19 particularly influenced this decision. The Company already had many AEC Regents and Regals, as well as AEC diesel engines fitted to SOS chassis, so was very familiar with AEC products. In the event, Trent's post war deckers until 1950 were not the Regent III model derived from the RT, but were of the pre-war derived Regent II type.

This superb picture at Ripley Market Place shows 1300, RA 7080, a 1928 Leyland bodied Leyland Lion PLSC3 acquired with the District Omnibus Service of G Phipps at Horsley Woodhouse in 1929. It remained in the fleet until 1934, and was photographed operating service 17, Belper-Ripley, via Heage and Openwoodgate.

BIBLIOGRAPHY

The following documents were used as original sources for my research:-

Records of the Trent Motor Traction Co, Ltd:-

Board Minute books.	Timetable Collection.
Rolling Stock Register.	Fleet records.
Ledgers.	Photographs.
Trent Bulletin	

Local Authority Minute Books at:-

Birmingham	Loughborough
Chesterfield	Luton
Derby	Mansfield
Doncaster	Nottingham
Ilkeston	Sheffield
Leicester	St Albans

Government Records at:

The Public Records Office, Kew, London.
Companies House, London Branch.
The British Library, Newspaper Library,
Colindale, London.

Museums and Photographic Collections:

Dennis, Guildford	National Motor Museum, Beaulieu
Reeve Burgess	Science Museum, London

Principal Newspapers and Journals

Alfreton and Belper Journal	Derbyshire Advertiser
Derby Evening Telegraph	Heanor Observer
Ilkeston Advertiser	Loughborough Echo
Nottingham Evening Post	Buses/Buses Illustrated
Commercial Motor	Motor Traction/Transport

ACKNOWLEDGMENTS

This book would not have been possible without the help and encouragement that I received with my research. I sought to record my thanks to my many helpers in Part One, and those thanks are again carried over into this volume. I must again, however, specifically record my thanks to the Chief Officials Team as listed in Part One for generously agreeing to allow me free access to Company records. Without that fundamental element of support, it is doubtful whether the project could ever have gone ahead. Many personalities have changed, and, in particular Brian King took over as General Manager in 1984 and kindly allowed my work to continue. I am also particularly grateful to Brian King for once again writing the Foreword to this volume in his capacity as Managing Director of Trent, and of the post privatisation holding Company, Wellglade. He made some helpful suggestions and his friendly support and encouragement has also been very much appreciated.

Trent staff who gave specific support and assistance with Part Two were Ian Francis and Malcolm Hitchin MBE. Fellow enthusiasts were always helpful, and these included Geoff Atkins, Peter Badgery, John Bennett, John Clarke, John Fooks, the late Stan Denton, Neville Evans, Philip Groves, Roy Marshall, David Stanier, Peter Taplin, Les Tuxford, Peter Yeomans and, of course, my publisher, Alan Oxley.

We are particularly fortunate in the East Midlands in having some of the most expert, active and knowledgeable enthusiast photographers, and their contribution to this volume must not be overlooked. Geoff Atkins, of course, began photographing buses at a very early stage, and was followed by Roy Marshall. Many people photograph buses today, but we are indeed richer for the pioneer work of both these two, and I specially wish to record my thanks to them for generously making their collections available for me to choose from. Peter Yeomans and Peter Badgery started a little later, but have also done much good work to record the transport scene, and I am grateful to them also for allowing me access to their work..

The Omnibus Society and PSV Circle have provided me with much information over the years, and I commend membership of these two bodies for those with a deeper interest in the subject.

Alan Mills, Malcolm Hitchin MBE and Roy Marshall kindly read the manuscript, and made a number of helpful suggestions, as did Alan Oxley. However, the responsibility for all interpretation, and any errors, rests entirely on my shoulders. My good friend, Dave McDonald, gave much help and support with the project over the years, and my son, Michael also helped with putting the work together.

PHOTOCREDITS

G H F Atkins 15, 27, 50, 55 (lower), 56, 58 (upper), 61 (upper, and lower left), 62 (upper right), 63 (upper and lower), 68 (upper), 75 (upper left), 86 (lower), 98, 148, 149 (lower right)

P Badgery 16, 25, 91 (lower right), 137 (lower)

D J Bean 67 (lower), 97 (upper left), 114, 115 (upper left), 131 (lower), 132 (left), 133 (right), 139

D J Bean Collection 14, 19, 20, 23, 26, 45, 49, 52 (lower right), 59 (upper right), 60 (upper and centre), 63 (centre), 65 (upper right), 66 (lower), 68 (lower), 70 (left), 71 (lower left), 72, 73 (upper left), 75 (right), 80 (lower left), 81, 83 (upper right), 86 (upper), 87 (upper), 88 (lower), 89 (lower), 92 (lower), 96 (lower), 100 (upper), 102 (lower), 106 (upper left, and lower), 124 (right)

M D Bean This page.

R Butler 149 (except lower right)

D Clark 8

Derby Evening Telegraph 150 (right)

Duple 103 (lower)

A Ingram 22

R Marshall 24, 29, 40, 42, 51, 54, 57 (upper), 58 (lower), 60 (lower left), 64,65 (centre and lower right), 66 (upper), 68 (centre), 71 (upper, 73 (lower), 74, 76 (upper), 77 (lower), 78, 79 (right), 80 (upper), 83 (upper left, and lower), 84 (left), 87 (lower), 88 (upper),89 (upper, 91 (upper), 93 (upper), 95 (upper), 96 (upper),97 (lower), 99 (upper), 101, 104, 105 (right), 106 (upper right), 107, 138 (lower), 140 (upper left)

Nottingham City Council, Central Library 136 (lower).

Omnibus Society 57

Photobus 37, 93 (lower)

H W Peers 33

RHG Simpson 13, 52 (upper right), 53 (upper), 55 (upper), 62 (lower left), 76 (lower), 105 (left)

E Surfleet 62 (upper left)

D J Stanier Collection 28, 38, 61 (lower right)

P Taplin 94

Trent 9, 11, 17, 18, 30, 31, 34, 41, 44, 48,52 (left), 53 (lower), 59 (except upper right), 66 (upper right), 69, 70 (right), 71 (lower right), 73 (upper right), 77 (upper), 79 (left), 80 (lower right), 84 (right), 90, 91 (lower left), 92 (upper), 94, 95 (lower), 97 (upper right), 99 (lower), 100 (lower), 102 (upper right), 113, 122, 123, 124 (left), 125, 126, 127,128, 129, 132 (right), 133 (left), 134, 135, 136 (upper), 137 (upper), 138 (upper), 140 (except upper left), 141 (except upper left), 142, 150(left).

W W Winter 130,131 (upper).

P Yeomans cover, 32, 67 (upper), 82, 102 (upper right), 103 (upper), 15 (except upper left), 116, 117, 141 (upper left)

THE AUTHOR

David Bean was born in Derby in 1948, and lived in Allestree until 1959. During this time, the buses of the Trent Motor Traction Co, Ltd kindled his interest in transport matters, and this led to a lifelong interest. Despite moving away from Derby, first to Croydon and later to Hertfordshire, where he still lives, he has maintained his interest in Trent throughout, with frequent visits to the Company's operating area.

A Chartered Engineer by profession, he was employed until recently as Director of Technical Services by St Albans City and District Council, but has now taken early retirement and works as a Consultant on Highways Traffic and Transport matters. Other interests are Do it Yourself, Photography, Walking and "struggling to keep fit!" He has two adult children.